AND A

KEYS TO MARRIAGE AND RELATIONSHIP SUCCESS

Copyright 2017
ISBN:9781944414252

KEYS TO MARRIAGE AND RELATIONSHIP SUCCESS
By Dr. David and Angela Burrows

UNLESS OTHERWISE STATED, all scripture references are from the New King James Version of the Bible. Copyright © 1982 by Thomas Nelson, Inc., publishers. Used by permission. All rights reserved.

Scriptures marked NIV taken from the New International Version®, NIV®. Copyright © 1973, 1978, 1984, 2011 by Biblica, Inc.™ Used by permission of Zondervan. All rights reserved worldwide, www.zondervan.com. The "NIV" and "New International Version" are trademarks registered in the United States Patent and Trademark Office by Biblica, Inc.™

Scriptural quotations are presented in italic font.

More Books on Marriage by Dr. Dave Burrows

- *Pleasing God in Relationships*
- *Sex and Dating,* Dr. Dave Burrows and Dr. Myles Munroe
- *How to Have the Best Sex (For Men Only)*
- *Who Let the Dogs Out?*

Other Books by Dr. Burrows

- *The Power of Positive Choices*
- *Leadership Lessons for Youth*
- *How to Publish Your Book*
- *How to Start a Business*
- *Transformational Leadership Lessons*
- *The Laws of GOOD SUCCESS*

Other resources available at:

www.daveburrowsinternational.com
www.sistersofsubstance.com
www.angelaburrows.com
www.bfmmm.com

Praise for Keys to Marriage and Relationship Success

DEDICATION

THIS BOOK IS dedicated to my "wifey for lifey" Angela "Angie" Burrows who has made our marriage experience one full of joy and fulfillment. Our journey has been one fantastic ride through joy, pain, understanding, learning, growth and fulfillment. Our marriage has given me hope for the institution of marriage and more specifically the original design of marriage by God. In a world that has altered and distorted the original our experience has taught us that the original is the best and when you know the true purpose of a thing you will not abuse it and you will find fulfillment. My prayer is that as you read this book and learn from our many years of experience it will enhance your marriage and put you in a position to provide wisdom and hope for others.

ANGELA BURROWS DEDICATION

I dedicate this publication to my Parents, Frank and Janet Dean who have provided an excellent example for me and countless others of what it is to truly love as Christ taught us to love. I also dedicate this project to my husband who has made my journey through the years of marriage a true delight. Finally i dedicate this project to the next generation, believing that what they will learn from us will ultimately lead to better relationships and marriages for years to come.

Contents

Dedication i

Introduction 1

CHAPTER 1: Affirming Divine Design: What Marriage Is Not 3

CHAPTER 2: Order 10

CHAPTER 3: Spirit First 17

CHAPTER 4: Understanding Needs 21

CHAPTER 5: Responsibility 28

CHAPTER 6: Acceptance 33

CHAPTER 7: Understanding 38

CHAPTER 8: Creating Good Habits 43

CHAPTER 9: Forgiveness 49

CHAPTER 10: Patience 56

CHAPTER 11: Anger 60

CHAPTER 12: Boundaries 68

CHAPTER 13: Communication 74

CHAPTER 14: Sex and Marriage 80

CHAPTER 15: Money 89

Semi-Final Words 93

Recommended Readings on Marriage 96

About the Authors 97

Introduction

Most of the people we consider normal desire to maintain successful relationships. If I took a survey of people who would like to have a terrible relationship or enjoy fighting or are hoping to get divorced or, better yet, would like to have a restraining order taken out against them, I would get no response across the board. This should tell us by default that virtually everyone wants a happy, long-term relationship. In the pages of this book we are going to discuss how to generate and maintain healthy relationships and, in particular, how to have a good marriage. We are going to provide some keys for you that we believe will help you build a strong and happy relationship.

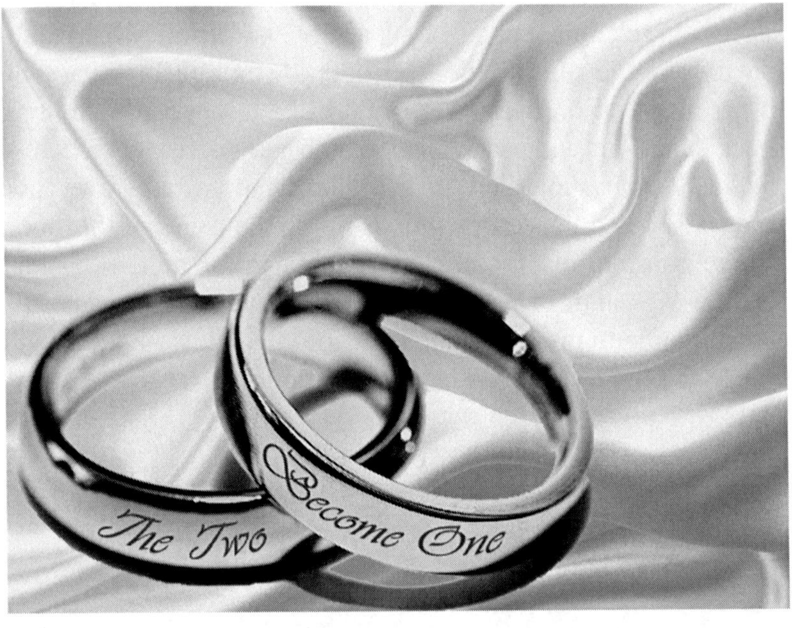
The Two
Become One

Chapter One

Affirming Divine Design: What Marriage Is Not

Today in our society and in the Body of Christ, there is steady erosion of the concepts and precepts of the Bible as they relate to both marriage and relationships. The erosion is systematic, subtle, and slow. It is like a ten-mile breeze rather than a hurricane. What seems to be happening in the society and in what we call the Body of Christ, or "The Kingdom," is that we are adopting alternatives to the original design. The norms of yesterday have been replaced by norms and morals and views that reflect the "new" philosophies of social scientists, "progressive thinkers," atheists, and a myriad of what we would consider to be worldly nonbiblical views.

We are seeing the emergence of new theologies that discount the original design in favor of new thinking that is based on what man feels makes sense rather than on the principles of the Bible which has been used as the basis of morals and laws for thousands of years. We have embarked on an era of compromising philosophies that have replaced the concept of original design with a new and confusing philosophy that contradicts and counteracts the concept of divine design. We have essentially adopted a very chaotic concept of relationships where there are no moral absolutes; whatever the majority accepts is what becomes the new social norm.

Having grown up in a time when it was a foregone conclusion that we are here not by any accident of nature but by divine design, the emerging relationship paradigms are clearly a compromise at best and confusing in the least. The new standards remind me so much of situational ethics, a system of morals that was very popular when I was coming out of high school. Situational ethics dictates that we do what is right for us at the moment, ignoring moral absolutes. This belief is unlike the biblical concept, where the values of the Bible are given to us and are firm, the principles and standards are fixed.

We need to realize that what we know as normal is being eroded. It appears to be a very systematic plan of the devil to create confusion and anarchy. The strategy is deliberate and it is definite. As people of God and as married persons and single persons, we must be aware of this; because if we are not, we may find ourselves agreeing with things that are being espoused by our friends and relatives and co-workers and others who have been exposed to these new philosophies. My perspective is that the Word of God must be the foundation of our morality if we call ourselves believers in Christ. It has to be. If not, what ends up happening is that we buy into a flawed philosophy that is based upon popular opinion. This is essentially what is happening in the world today: There is a flawed philosophy going around presenting itself as truth. There's a philosophy going around that says marriage is outside of God, it does not relate to God, and we can create any arrangement and call it marriage. That's a flawed perception.

I want to begin with an overview. First, marriage is God's design. God invented marriage. Marriage is the foundation of a stable society. You cannot have a stable society without successful marriages. We are seeing the results of failed marriages around us every day. Whenever the family is messed up, society is messed up. They simply go hand in hand. When we examine what is wrong in the world today, we find that most addicts, offenders, sexually and psychologically abused persons are from dysfunctional homes and the majority of dysfunctional homes are fatherless homes.

- **85% of all youths in prison come from fatherless homes (Source: Fulton Co. Georgia jail populations, Texas Dept. of Corrections 1992) – 20 times the [national?] average.**

- **71% of all high school dropouts come from fatherless homes (Source: National Principals Association Report on the State of High Schools) – 9 times the [national?] average.**

- **90% of all homeless and runaway children are from fatherless homes – 32 times the [national?] average.**

- **63% of youth suicides are from fatherless homes (Source: U.S. D.H.H.S., Bureau of the Census) – 5 times the [national?] average.**

- **70% of youths in state-operated institutions come from fatherless homes (Source: U.S. Dept. of Justice, Special Report, Sept. 1988)– 9 times the [national?] average.**

According to the Bible, marriage was designed by God as a covenant between a man and a woman; that's the original design. Now, I know that people like to make amendments to original constitutions. However, we cannot make amendments to the Bible, because the Bible was written by God through men and is already concluded; there are no further amendments to be made. Since God has declared that marriage is between a man and a woman, we cannot use the Bible to validate any other kind of marriage arrangement; it is impossible. There is nothing to debate. (Even if you are not using the Bible, the alternatives to God's design still do not make logical sense to me; but I cannot speak for people who are using their own philosophy.)

The Bible also says that marriage is **honorable,** which means it is a good thing to get into. Today, we have a lot of people who feel that marriage is dishonorable. Young people in particular shy away from marriage as if it were something to be wary of. Many people blame marriage for heartbreak, disappointment and undue suffering. The people who enter into marriage may not be honorable, but marriage itself will always be honorable. The problem may be that we are blaming the institution of marriage for a plethora of issues when it is actually the people who get married who are to blame. You cannot blame marriage when you have dishonorable people who are married; because when dishonorable people get married, they dishonor marriage. Consider this: Reckless and drunk drivers kill thousands of people every year; the cars never kill anyone, the drivers do. In the same way, marriage is a fully functional vehicle, but it needs to be properly managed and handled otherwise it can cause serious destruction.

You should not judge marriage by your experience with it. You should judge marriage by its original design and purpose. You should judge marriage through the eyes of its originator. God ordained marriage; therefore we have to assess marriage based on His standards. Hebrews 13:4 says: *Marriage is honorable among all and the bed is undefiled: but fornicators and adulterers God will judge.* This is God's word. Our biblical constitution establishes that "marriage is honorable" and "the bed is undefiled." In other words, marriage is a good thing and you and your spouse have a license to do anything that you want to do in the bedroom (within reason).

In order to have successful relationships we have to understand the design of marriage. So let's talk a little bit about that. Genesis

2:23 says: *This is now bone of my bone and flesh of my flesh. She shall be called woman because she was taken out of man.* These are Adam's words. Then God says: *Therefore, a man shall leave his father and mother and be joined to his wife.* Now, you'll notice the instruction is very specific: It says he leaves his father and mother; that rules out any other arrangement. You cannot leave your father and a dog. You cannot leave your father and another father. It has to be that you leave your father and mother and be joined to your wife. And, in the Bible a wife is a woman and a husband is a man.

I know there's a tremendous movement in the world to kill marriage as we know it, and in the process to shut down the church as we know it and replace it with a new manmade, state-run model that cannot be found in the Bible. When the church talks about marriage now, a lot of people become offended. Can you imagine that? The original design of marriage is now offensive to people. People get angry at you because you say, "I believe in traditional marriage." Why is it offensive to believe that there is an original design and the original design is the best and the way it should be? It is remarkable to me that we have come to the point where, if you espouse the original, you are accused of hate speech. I am personally baffled by this! If I say I appreciate the original, why should you become angry at me? If *you* decide to make an amendment and you decide that you want to do things another way, that's up to you; do not get mad at me. And do not ask the Bible to sanction your decision; you're wasting your time. You cannot find another definition for marriage anywhere in the Bible. You may be able to find it in a comic book or some other book, but you cannot find it in the Bible. The scripture says: *And they were both naked and the man and his wife were not ashamed*—this is the original design. God designed man and wife to be together in marriage and He said it is honorable.

If marriage is good, honorable and essential to a stable society, then we must identify and embrace the keys to marriage success.

If marriage is essential for the success of our society, then we need to figure out how to make it work.

I want to begin by talking about what makes a good marriage and by telling you the results of successful marriages. But, first, let me make this point: Better marriages mean better children. When children do not have a father as an example, or a mother as an example, they are deficient. They come into the world deficient because marriage was designed for children to see what they are supposed to be like. Successful marriage gives young people an image of the future. It gives them a guideline so that they know—and do not have to figure out—how to act. They do not have to figure out how to love. They see their father and mother and they get all the information they need from that relationship. So, better marriages mean better children. Better children mean better students, better employees, and better citizens. Our world just works better when marriages are good. That's the truth of the matter. When we have better marriages, we have less dysfunction, we have less crime and less murder, and we have less mayhem. In fact, if all marriages were good, we wouldn't have any problems. When we have successful children, those children grow up to become the husbands and wives who repeat the process. Therefore, marriage is essential to our future.

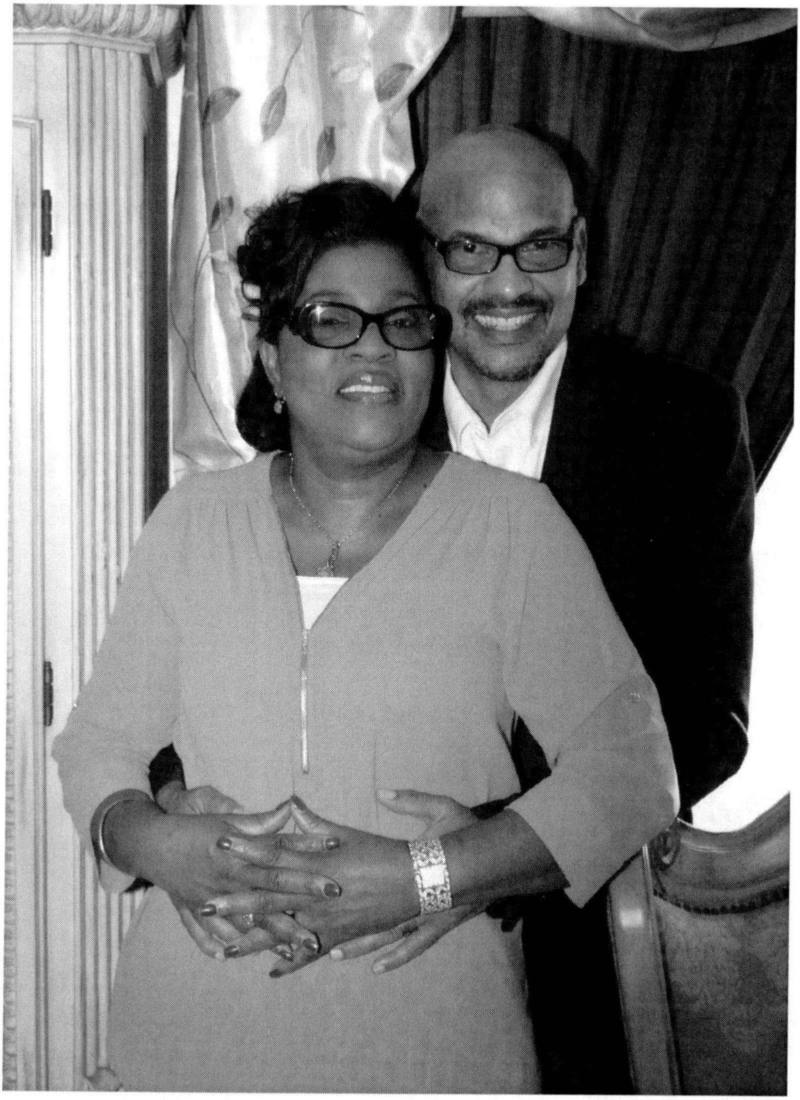

CHAPTER TWO

ORDER

THE FIRST KEY to marriage is **order.** The late Dr. Myles Munroe, my dear friend and mentor, used to say, "If you do not know the purpose of the thing, you will abuse it." Purpose really is original order, or original design.

Here's what the Bible says about order in marriage.

> *Wives, submit to your own husbands, as to the Lord. For the husband is head of the wife, as also Christ is head of the church; and He is the Savior of the body. Therefore, just as the church is subject to Christ, so let the wives be to their own husbands in everything.*
>
> *Husbands, love your wives, just as Christ also loved the church and gave Himself for her, that He might sanctify and cleanse her with the washing of water by the word, that He might present her to Himself a glorious church, not having spot or wrinkle or any such thing, but that she should be holy and without blemish. So husbands ought to love their own wives as their own bodies; he who loves his wife loves himself. For no one ever hated his own flesh, but nourishes and cherishes it, just as the Lord does the church.*
>
> *—Ephesians 5:22-29*

Now, sometimes when we look at a scripture like this one, it can seem like a prison. We have to understand, however, what God is trying to communicate when He describes this order. God says that in order for things to work, somebody has to be the head and somebody has to be the assistant. You cannot have two heads. Whenever you have two heads, you have a problem; you have a monster, really. God never says that the husband was the smarter one, or superior in any way; He simply says this is the way things work best. And when God talks about leadership and roles within the marriage, He is saying that things work best when the wife recognizes the position—office—of the husband. You are not to look at the person occupying the office; you look at what the office was designed to do. We have had good and bad Presidents; but that does not mean we eliminate the office because the person occupying it has done a poor job or has abused the office. And that's the crux of the discussion. When the Bible talks about submission, it means submitting to the authority of the position not necessarily the person. The position of husband, according to God, is the position of leader: we cannot argue with this. People who do argue with this point usually do not have a successful track record. The validity of your speech should be your performance. In my humble estimation, the results prove that God's design works best. When you have two-headed teams, you always have problems because nobody is in charge.

What is interesting is that God says later in the passage from Ephesians: *Husbands, love your wives* (v25). Sometimes husbands miss this part of the marriage order because they read the first part and conclude, "Well, you know what, the Bible says I am in charge." Men tend to use this statement to lord themselves over women. But the truth of the matter is, men only possess **positional authority.** This means a husband is not relationally in authority in the sense that he has total authority over his wife. The husband's authority comes from the office; and to hold the office legitimately, he must conform to the rules of the office. The husband cannot require his wife to do what God says and fail himself to do what God says. They go hand in hand. Therefore, this scripture is saying to husbands, you are in charge and here is your first command: Love your wife. Now, if you do not love your wife, you diminish your authority.

The scripture goes even further to say: *Love your wives, just as Christ also loved the church and gave Himself for her.* For the husband to be legitimate in his position of authority, he must love his wife as Christ loved the church. If he does not love as Christ loved the church, then his authority is compromised. You see, this thing only works according to God's plan. If you say the husband is the head of the wife, but the husband does not have a relationship with God, that's a problem, because the husband is not going to be able to fulfill the commands.

The passage continues: *Husbands, love your wives, just as Christ also loved the church and gave Himself for her,* **that He might sanctify and cleanse her with the washing of water by the word** (v26, bold added). What does this mean? A man is supposed to know the Word. When you say that you are in authority in your marriage and you want your wife to submit to you, the Bible says that when she submits to you, first, you have to love her, and second, you have to know the Word and you have to wash her by the Word. It is clear, then, that there are requirements for this position of authority. It is not blanket authority; God is not saying to men you're in charge, so do whatever you want to do. He is saying that He has put you in a position of authority and here is how you need to behave in this position. The scripture continues: *that He might present her to Himself a glorious church, not having spot or wrinkle or any such thing, but that she should be holy and without blemish* (v27). So, when you lead as the Bible instructs, you cause your wife to be refined—*holy and without blemish.*

The often-misquoted passage that husbands ought to love their own wives is not talking about men being in charge of women, it is about husbands being in a position of authority in the marriage. So do not say, "Because I am a man, I am in charge." No, being a

Order

man does not qualify you for anything. Being a **husband** qualifies you to exercise authority; and even then, there are qualifications within the qualification. Interestingly enough, the scripture goes on to specify: *So husbands ought to love their **own** wives as their own bodies* (v28a, bold added). I do not know why that word *own* was put in there, but it is a very important word. Men are commanded to love their **own** wives. This command suggests that some brothers do not know how to love their own wives because they are busy trying to love someone else's wife. The command even says that husbands are to love their own wives *as their own bodies*. In other words, a husband is supposed to love his wife in the same way he would treat his body. It makes sense that *he who loves his wife loves himself* (v28b). So, if you do not love your wife, you are showing that you do not love yourself. In order for me to truly love myself, I have to love my wife. If I do not love my wife, I do not love myself. According to God, that is the end of the story.

The scripture continues: *For no one ever hated his own flesh but nourishes it and cherishes it* (v29). Men have a responsibility to nourish and to cherish, just as the Lord nourishes and cherishes the Church. *For we are members of His body, of His flesh and of His bones. "For this reason a man shall leave his father and mother and be joined to his wife, and the two shall become one flesh." This is a great mystery, but I speak concerning Christ and the church. Nevertheless let each one of you in particular so love his own wife as himself, and let the wife see that she respects her husband.* Now, what I want you to notice in this passage is that God commands husbands to love their wives; but it does not command wives to love their husbands. Do you think God does not want the wife to love the husband? Of course not. He wants her to love her husband but He emphasized the things that relate to the characteristics and nature of the male person and the female person. What do women need most? Women need love. What do men need most? Men need respect. So He says to husbands, love your wives, and to wives, respect your husband. A man needs respect as a primary fulfillment. A woman needs love as a primary fulfillment. It does not mean that both do not need love; it just means that a woman is created, wired and designed for love. She is made for romance. God is like a master programmer: He has programmed men and women with characteristics that fit their physiological or biological design. Is it not amazing that sperm is not visible except under a microscope yet it contains your DNA and all the programming that relates to you that will not be visible for years to come. The programming of God is amazing!

We conducted a survey during one of our marriage ministry sessions. We asked the married couples what was required in a marriage. Fifty percent (50%) of the women and only two percent (2%) of the men answered romance. That big difference in value reflects that a woman has a natural design that causes her to be emotional and needing of love and desiring romance. A man does not really need romance; it is is good to a man but it is not essential. But to a woman, romance is absolutely essential. God made man and woman to be different, and each one has a separate and distinct role. The need for love, for romance is the natural God-given makeup of a woman. When this need is not satisfied, according to original design it is called an abnormality.

PASTOR ANGIE:
> I attended a wedding where the people were having such a good time even though many of them did not have a close relationship with the Lord, as we would characterize it. When the time came for people to leave, they kept singing and didn't want to go home; so the operators had to turn off the music. There I was, enjoying it all. I said to myself it is a wonderful thing to be married, even if the marriage is not perfect. The very idea of marriage is a beautiful thing: two persons pledging their love and committing to care for each other for life. That is a beautiful thing that is made even more special when you understand the original design and purpose of marriage.

Order is so essential. When we are operating outside of the programmed design and we begin to accept and adopt the alterations, we end up with a flawed philosophy that produces flawed relationships and flawed marriages. So, foundationally, I want us as believers to be mindful of the importance of the Word of God in everything we do. Remember that being a person of standard who is aligned with God's laws means that many times—as I will show—you may be considered the odd person out. But the Bible already has declared that you would be the odd person out; so do not get flustered or disturbed when people do not understand why you would adhere to biblical, Godly design and roles in your marriage. You may ask, "Why is that so?" The Word says that few go on the narrow road and there are many on the broad road (Matthew 7:13-14); so, as a Christian, as a woman of God, as a wife, you cannot focus on what everyone else is doing. It is okay to be the odd person out because you're going to be judged on the Word rather than on popular opinion.

Let me interject something in case some of us have forgotten. We must remember that this arena and this area, the terra firma that we're living on today, the earth, is a temporary place. This is not what is going to be. According to God, we are spirits; our physical bodies are residing here and one day, believe it or not, we are going to account for every deed done in the body, every deed. I thought about this a few years ago, and I said, "Lord God, we are going to have to give an account for every deed. And with that thought in mind, Lord, I want to live in line with your laws and if I have done negative deeds, I want to start doing good deeds." I have to do good to my husband and fulfill my designed role because God is going to judge me by my adherence to His plan for me as a woman and a wife. That is why I try not to engage my tongue, even in certain conversations. I prefer to walk away so that my deeds may remain good. I respect my husband because that is what the Word of God says. He loves me because it is my primary need and I respect him because it is his primary need.

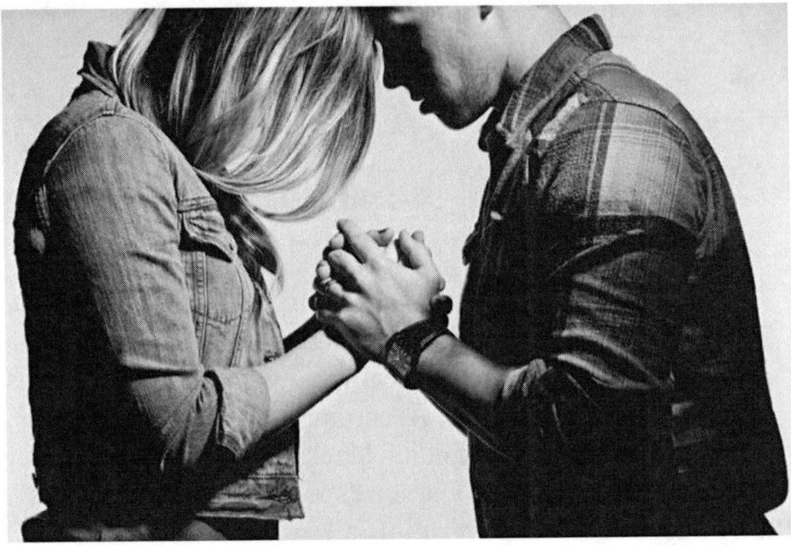

Chapter Three

Spirit First

Pastor Angie:

As married people, we must be cognizant that there must be a third person in our marriage constantly. When we think of marriage from a purely natural standpoint, we are thinking of two persons involved in a relationship. But God tells us that we have physical bodies yet we are not just physical. We have come from an unseen world into a seen world; but the unseen preexisted the seen and is more powerful than the seen. So we should recognize that we are more than what we see. Spirits are not visible, only flesh is. Our marriages should begin in the Spirit and then be expressed in the flesh. If we begin in the Spirit, then that third person must also be in the bedroom. That Person is the Holy Spirit.

Many of us can believe God for money, or for a car or house, or for a scholarship to attend college. But we find it difficult to believe God for healing and restoration in our relationships. If you are having trouble in your marriage today, use your faith—have the same faith that you would use to believe to get a new car or that new house—and believe God to intervene in your marriage. The Holy Spirit is our paraclete; He is called to be alongside to help us.

Marriage within the Body of Christ should be more beautiful, more enjoyable than marriage outside the Body of Christ. A marriage that is spiritual first should never be a bad relationship that you have to endure. The Spirit-first marriage should be the most amazing, beautiful, fulfilling, fun, adventuresome, fantastic, sexy (God invented sex so there is nothing wrong with being sexy TO YOUR HUSBAND) marriage. Your marriage will never be perfect; I know that you have challenges and differences in personality, but those are realities of life in an imperfect world. Despite shortcomings and frailties, when you submit your will to the Holy Spirit, watch your marriage become a beautiful thing. You do not have to believe the adage that two persons have to be exactly alike for the marriage to be successful. My husband and I are not alike, but we have a great time. I am not saying that to impress you; I truly love my husband and he truly loves me. And to add to that, I also like him! I do not just love him, I like him, which is really important.

PASTOR DAVE:

I agree that marriage should be Spirit-based first. If your marriage is based in the flesh, the Bible says the flesh will fail you. Your flesh can be problematic at times. When you trust your flesh, you get into all kinds of problems; but if you begin in the Spirit, then you can conquer the issues of the flesh. The flesh has all kinds of problems. Your body desires the wrong things. If you allow your body to do whatever it would like to do, it would kill you. Your body would drink rum, use cocaine, run with bad women, all kinds of stuff, because of our sin nature; that is what we are naturally inclined to do. And this is why we need the Spirit. And this is why marriage must be Spirit-based first. I have been married for years, but my flesh has not changed. If I do not stay in the Spirit, the issues of my past will come back and destroy my marriage. My history is not a good one when it comes to relationships, before I submitted to God. I was in multiple relationships as a youth—abusive, lust-filled, promiscuous relationships—that were very selfish. I had to overcome my past and decide to submit to the plan of God for my life and enter a Spirit-led marriage. My submission to the Holy Spirit has meant that I have overcome the temptation for multiple relationships and lust-filled trysts and have entered into something beautiful and exclusive with this wonderful woman. She is all I need now; and I can say that only because we both have a Spirit-first marriage concept. The flesh leads ultimately to death; the Spirit leads to and produces life, joy and peace. Be Spirit-led and Spirit-first in your marriage.

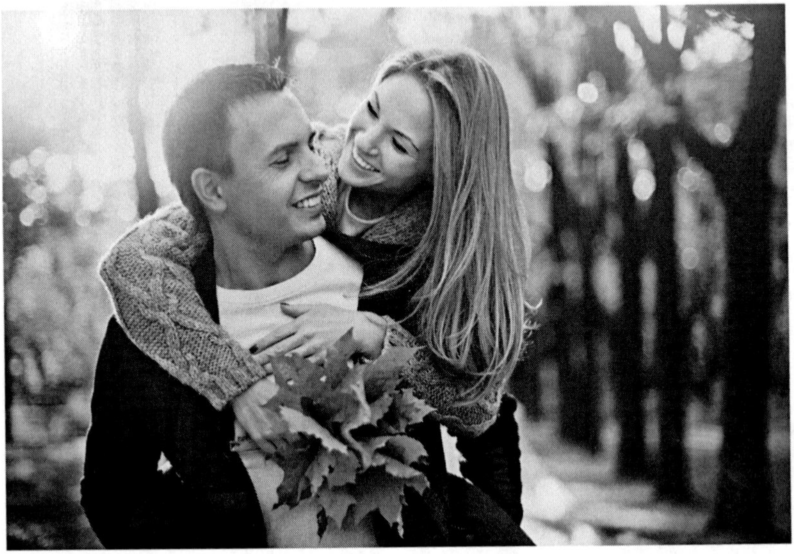

CHAPTER FOUR

UNDERSTANDING NEEDS

PASTOR DAVE:

WHAT DO MEN and woman need? It is imperative in marriage, and in all relationships, that we try to understand what the other person needs. This knowledge is pivotal because if we do not understand our needs and these needs go unmet, we create deficiencies in the relationship. As we mentioned earlier, a woman needs primarily to be loved. A man needs primarily to be respected. Now we will take a deeper look at the differences in our makeup so we can determine how to meet those needs.

Women, you have to remind yourselves that a man does not need what you need. Sometimes, as a woman you may wonder: "Why doesn't he feel the way I feel?" It's because he's a man. By the same token, men, you should understand that a woman does not need what you need. Men often think: "Okay, well, as soon as a woman looks at me, she wants to have sex." That's not the way women are made up; so you should not expect a woman to feel and appreciate what you feel and appreciate; men and women are made different. A man likes to feel that he is respected. One of the worst things that can happen to a man is to feel he is not a "man in his own house." A man who feels disrespected by his wife is experiencing a deficiency. By the same token, a woman who feels unloved by her husband is also experiencing a deficiency.

AFFECTION (NOT NECESSARILY SEX)

PASTOR ANGIE:
Women, for the most part, are more affectionate creatures than men; they are wired that way. Women have more nerve endings; therefore physical touch is extremely important to them. Take, for example, holding hands: Women are more sensitive than men and enjoy the experience of feeling connected, so women like to hold hands in public. Men, however, might feel uncomfortable with holding hands. They are frequently embarrassed by public displays of affection. They say to themselves: "My boys can see me. They're going to call me soft." If you are a man who does not understand women, then you might buy into that sentiment; but when you understand women, you understand the importance of physical touch. Women like to be touched—and not necessarily sexually. A common complaint among married women is: "My husband does not touch me unless he wants sex." The thinking of most men is: "She's touching me, jackpot!" Touching without sexual intent is a hard thing for men to navigate because they think and feel differently. A man likes to touch, but he likes to touch for a particular purpose.

PASTOR DAVE:
I want to tell you a story about physical touch. A couple was having problems, so they went to a therapist. The husband and wife each described the problem.

> The wife said: "My husband does not touch me. He never hugs me, you know. I do not have any physical evidence of his love."
>
> The husband said: "Well, you know, I told you I loved you when we were married. I didn't change my mind."

Understanding Needs

As they went on with the therapist, they started to explore ways of improving their marriage. Finally, after talking to both, the therapist said, "You know what? I've figured out what the problem is." He asked the husband, "Do I have permission to show you something that can change your marriage?" The husband answered, "Sure, you go right ahead." The therapist asked the wife to stand up and said to her, "Come here, give me a hug," and he gave the wife a hug. As soon as the therapist hugged her, she started smiling. He looked at the husband and said, "That's one of your biggest problems. Sometimes all your wife needs is a hug. Do you get it?" The husband answered, "Yes, I get it." "So, you agree with it?" the therapist pressed. The husband responded, "Yes. I see that that works so well. So, what time should I bring her back next week?"

Pastor Angie:

He really didn't get it, huh? What a sad case! Even though this is a joke, it does illustrate that some men are stuck in their minds; they are stuck in a mode of thinking. And maybe some women are stuck in a mode of thinking too. What do I mean by stuck? I simply mean that we declare: "This is my personality and this is who I am, and I am not changing. This is how he married me or this is how she married me." But you are adaptable. You can adapt. Psychologists say that we change every five years. Do you know why we change? The experiences of life change us. To be honest, my husband and I are not the young happy-go-lucky persons we were when we got married. We still find those happy-go-lucky moments in there, but dealing with the vicissitudes of life has changed us. When we first got married, everything—I mean everything—was exciting. We were so excited about one another, we used to meet at home at lunch time. That is how excited we were to see each other. I know what some of you are thinking....We simply loved being together!

As you get older and acquire other responsibilities, you find you have less and less time for things like that. Particularly when you have children, you find it difficult to share that time as a couple. But you must keep the embers burning in your love. You have to remember each other's makeup and needs.

Men, make an effort to learn your wife's love language, and speak it fluently. Every woman is different and loves differently. In his book The 5 Love Languages: The Secret to Love That Lasts, Gary Chapman states that there are five love languages. The five are: quality time, physical touch, acts of service, gifts, and words of affirmation. Some of us have primary love languages. It is also important to know this information know for your children, because children have love languages too and you have to learn to speak to that as well. Your siblings and your parents have love languages.

It is really important, men, to find out what your wife's preferred manner of expressing love is and to make a conscious effort to love her in that way. The same admonishment goes for wives. Study what makes your husband feel most respected and loved, and try to make those things happen. Make sure you understand each other's love language and constantly remind yourself about your spouse's love language.

If you can identify each other's love languages, you would save yourself a lot of work and increase the likelihood of harmony and satisfaction in your marriage. If your love tank is full, you would not be tempted to fill up elsewhere, whether it be at work or at church or wherever someone recognizes your love language and inadvertently or intentionally attempts to fill your tank. We want glorious relationships. You want to see heaven on earth in your marriage. I say heaven on earth because we want to bring the nature and precepts of the Kingdom of God into our relationships. People outside the kingdom have painted a picture of marriage as being nothing but effortless, passionate sex or nothing but trouble. Marriage will always

Understanding Needs

have its challenges; but the challenges are minimized when we learn to love each other and communicate effectively.

People make jokes about the three rings in marriage—the **engagement ring**, the **wedding ring**, and the **suffer-ring**. In fairness, it sounds funny, but we should not allow such jokes to take root in our mind because we speak things into the atmosphere. We have to be conscious about what we are declaring over our loved ones and relationships. I speak that my husband loves me as Christ loves the church. And I will honor him and I will respect him, even when I have a difference of opinion. I choose to honor my man because when he feels good then my home life is better.

A few weeks ago, when my son was home for the weekend to attend a wedding, he said to me: "Mommy, I am leaving, I am going home." I responded: "Okay." Then he said: "Yes, Mommy, but you need to go home, because you know how Daddy gets when you're not home….like when I am out too late." So I said: "Yes, you all stay, I am going home."

The night before that, on a Friday night, my son and I were speaking outside my bedroom door. (He and I are the long-winded persons in my family.) It was late, about midnight or so, and my husband had gone to bed. Then my son said, "Mommy, you better go to bed, Daddy is grumbling." Grumbling means: "Stop talking outside my door; I am ready for my sleep!" I hope you recognize from this reflection the importance of the love languages. They are critical for effective communication, understanding and amicable relationships.

When it comes to needs, husbands and wives, pay attention to these five things and discover what love languages your spouse speaks. Even if it is not your spouse—if it is your prospective spouse, your boyfriend, your girlfriend, or your friend—learn the other person's love languages, because love languages are essential to the success of your marriage, any relationship.

Pastor Dave:

I learned certain things about my wife when I became her husband; and as I learned those things, I had to remind myself of them. My wife loves quality time and she loves words of affirmation. She really likes all the love languages, but I know she loves quality time. Sometimes my wife would call me to say she wants to see me and wants me to spend time with her, and I think: "If you call me home there'd better be something special in it for me." But she just wants that time of us being together. It may not make sense to me but I have to realize it makes sense to her and if I want her to recognize my needs, I need to recognize her needs. It goes back to the principle of sowing and reaping: Whatever you sow, you reap (Galatians 6:7). It also goes back to the Golden Rule: Do unto others as you would have them do unto you (Matthew 7:12; Luke 6:31). If I want my needs met, I have to meet her needs.

It is not difficult for us to keep track of our own needs because we are constantly aware of them. When we're in a marriage relationship, however, we have to remind ourselves of the other person's needs and make sure to address them.

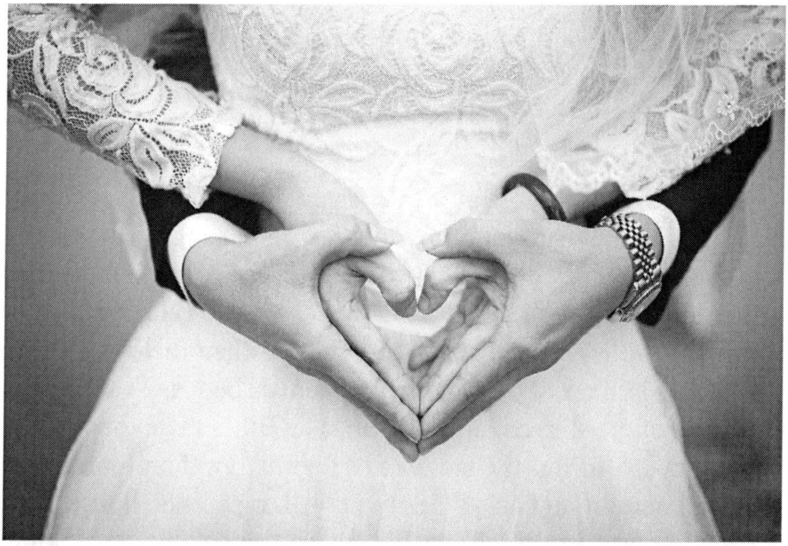

Chapter Five

RESPONSIBILITY

PASTOR DAVE:

I AM GOING to speak from a man's perspective right now about something that is pivotal to a successful marriage. That matter is responsibility. Men, a captain never leaves the ship. A man should never say "I am leaving," because the **relation** is your **ship.** If the woman gives up and leaves, then that's different; but you should not be the one who leaves because you are the captain of the ship called *Relation*. The Bible says you find her and leave your family and take her with you; therefore, if you picked her out and asked her to leave her parents' house, then you are responsible for her. If you are responsible you cannot abandon ship, no matter what happens.

Can you imagine being onboard a ship and when the seas become rough the captain says, "Sorry, I am going to get off and you all can stay on the boat"? Pretty ridiculous, right? In the same way, a man is never supposed to leave the ship: that ought to be your mentality as a man. That's why God says "you're in charge." If you are in charge, you cannot leave. You cannot have the chief executive of the office saying, "Man, things are too rough in this company. I am gone." You are the leader. As husband you have responsibility and you have

Responsibility

to take responsibility for everyone on the ship—the wife, the children, everybody.

When you're on a plane, the pilot is responsible for everybody on the plane. It is the same way in a marriage. The husband is the pilot, the wife is the co-pilot. But the pilot is ultimately in charge because he is also in charge of the co-pilot, even though the co-pilot can do everything that he can do. But his position of authority puts him in the position where he is in charge. Men, you have to think that way.

A captain prepares for challenges. Challenges will come in a relationship. And if you are under some illusion that you will not have difficulties, you will not adequately prepare yourself for those challenges. As a man, you have to prepare yourself for challenges. You have to recognize that there are going to be times when your wife is going to disagree with you; times when she is going to be angry; times when she is going to feel like leaving you. And then you're going to have personal challenges. Life is a challenge; just being a Christian is a challenge; being good is a challenge; everything is a challenge. I want to direct your attention to a scripture in the book of Job that tells us about challenges. Job describes the challenging aspect of life, specifically as it relates to men. (This passage does not refer only to men, but I want men to get this.) Job 14:1 reads: *Man who is born of woman / Is of few days and full of trouble.* Notice that the verse says man has to be born of woman; if you are born of something else (other than woman), then you are not a man, but we are all born into this world through a woman so this statement refers to all men. Trouble means difficulties, complex issues and problems. So, as a man you have to prepare for trouble. But later in the Scriptures, Jesus says: *In the world you will have tribulation; but be of good cheer, I have overcome the world* (John 16:33). Men, you have to realize that trouble is coming, but through the Holy Spirit you are prepared to deal with the trouble.

PASTOR ANGIE:

As a female, I'd like to chime in and say that as a man you need to be spiritually in tune with what is going on in your house. I say this because sometimes your wife may argue with you because she disagrees with you; but other times she might be under demonic attack. And, as a man of God, you need to have yourself centered in the spiritual climate in your home so that you can see if there is something going on with your wife that is not normal. She is not just disagreeing with you because she does not agree; maybe she is being influenced or she is being stressed out at work. At such times, you, as a man, must take authority: You declare in your house what spirit is going to operate in your house and you decide to act or demand those spirits to leave.

The same advice applies for women. Sometimes your husband might answer you in a way that is not like him. It may not be because he has so much to do or is overwhelmed right then; he might be under demonic attack. Therefore, you have to pray the Word of God over your husband and you have to declare that Satan has no place in your residence, that Satan has no place in your marriage, and that Satan has no place messing with your children. I do not care what manifestations you see: You declare. We tend to look just at the natural. Yes, marriage is natural, but there are spiritual forces that are at work in the real world. The devil hates marriage and that is why there is so much nonsense about marriage in the world. In case you didn't know it, people of God, the younger generation, particularly in North America, believes a lot of that nonsense—foolishness, flawed philosophies—about marriage. Our children are exposed to these "new" philosophies and they come to us with weird ideas. We do not know a lot about what our children believe; so we must take authority to ensure we do not tolerate the wrong spirits affecting their lives.

Sometimes you have to say: "That's not my character, that's not me, that's not the way I believe or behave" and take

Responsibility

authority. Sometimes you have to recognize disorder and deal with it creatively. Once I sent my husband a song. It was not a Christian song but the lyrics stuck with me. I felt at the time that if I spoke the lyrics to him, he would not get the message, so I simply emailed it to him. The song was "There's a Stranger in My House." It took a while for him to figure out why I had sent him a song, but as he listened to the lyrics the reason became clear. The chorus said:

> There's a stranger in my house
> It took a while to figure out
> There's no way you could be who you say you are
> You gotta be someone else
> Cuz he wouldn't touch me like that
> And he wouldn't treat me like you do
> He would adore me, he wouldn't ignore me
> So I'm convinced there's a stranger in my house

I sent him that song because he was acting unlike himself. For about two weeks I was feeling that "This is not my husband. My husband does not speak to me like this; he does not touch me like that"; so, I sent him the song. His reaction was, "What is this?" I replied, "Honey, you are not yourself." You have to let your spouse know when they are behaving out of character; and you also have to know if the strange behavior is due to some spiritual influence. And you take authority over it.

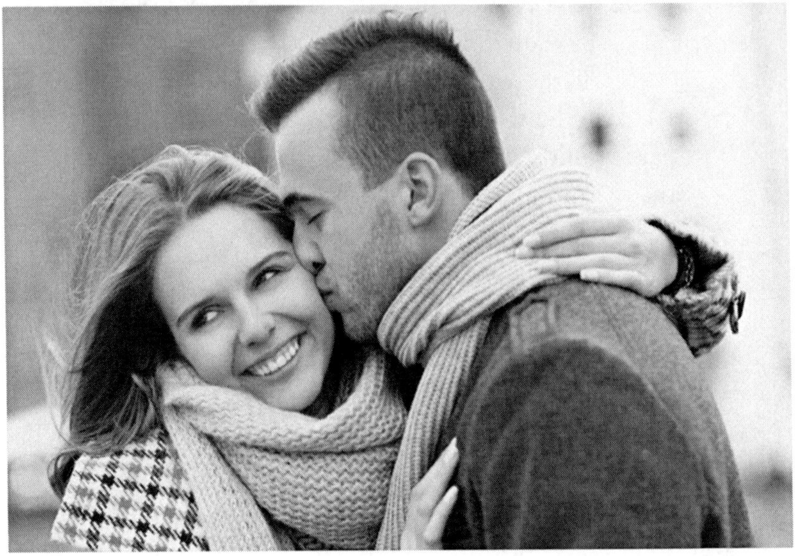

Chapter Six

ACCEPTANCE

PASTOR DAVE:

THE NEXT KEY to successful relationships is acceptance. This is really important. In fact, acceptance is the most important building block of your marriage. If you choose to marry someone based upon what you **want** them to **become**, then you will never **really** accept them. You have to begin where you are. You have to begin with all of their faults. You have to learn to accept each other, including all of your own faults. When you can accept a person fully, then, and only then, can the two of you correct and build a better relationship. If you do not accept a person for who they are, then the two of you cannot even build, because you are constantly disappointed and disillusioned with each other even at the beginning. Therefore, you have to learn how to accept one another.

If you never accept the person you've married, you'll never be happy with your spouse. If you do not accept your spouse as they are, then you never give them an opportunity to make mistakes and grow. It is important to remember that you chose your spouse; you decided that you want to marry that person. You should not then decide that you don't accept the person you've married. You have to accept them as they are. Some people are untidy, some people are noisy, some people snore, and there are all other kinds of issues. Accept your spouse—issues and all—because we all have issues.

There is a song by Billy Joel that used to be played on the radio years ago; it went like this: "Don't go changing, to try and please me...I love you just the way you are." You really have to adopt that attitude in your relationships. If you do not love your spouse just the way they are, they will not become what you want them to be. We have to understand that a successful marriage is all about accepting a person and loving them right where they are. Therefore, I have to accept my wife with all of her faults and all of her issues (I know she does not have any, but I have to accept them, nonetheless). We all have faults which, many times, we cannot see; and that's a part of the problem.

Once we accept each other just the way we are, the next step is to realize that change can happen. But change does not happen overnight. We have to find and fight our way through the process of change. Sometimes major changes will never happen; so if we only accept each other based upon changes we expect to see, our relationship will fail. Find a way to be content with your spouse even if they never make the changes you want to see. Recognize that over time we will all make changes.

Pastor Angie:

I want to say something to husbands on behalf of women. It is amazing to me that a husband would complain about his wife; for example, about how she's not very tidy. Instead of criticizing her, perhaps you can teach her how you would like things to be and help her to fix them. I know that sometimes it's hard for people to get rid of habits that can get on one's nerves. But just because we do not struggle with an issue does not mean we have the right to look down on the spouse who is struggling with the issue.

It is also ridiculous to me that a man would compare his wife to another woman. That is just ludicrous to me. You should never do that. You should never compare your wife to another woman. Women are particularly sensitive creatures; and I know that many of us struggle with insecurity. Therefore, comparing your wife to someone else only serves to humiliate her, and make her feel inferior and angry at you and the person to whom you're comparing her. Over the years, I've watched so many men talk about their wife's weight but do nothing to actually help her get or stay in shape. I told one man, "That's your fault. You should take her walking. You should take her jogging. You're supposed to invest in what you want to see in your wife." You might say you do not like the way your wife speaks. Well, invest in a course; send her to Toastmasters; perhaps just give her a tutor; or buy her some elocution software to use on her computer. You're supposed to be the answer to her problem. Why? You love her as Christ loves the church. What did Christ do? He gave himself. Men, your nature, your anatomy is giving. Your spirit—the spiritual man—is giving. If you nurture this woman right, what you'll get back is so awesome! It is so awesome!

Sometimes I do not need a hug from my husband, I just need to be to reminded of a scripture to help me get through one of those days when I've got twenty things to do and a few minutes to do them. Just wash me with the Word of God. Sometimes women just need the Word. We just need to be reminded—and not in a berating manner—of a scripture. So men, sometimes the reason some of you have the problems you are experiencing in your home and with your wife is because you are not feeding her soul. You have to uplift, enlighten and encourage her so she can become all she can be. Remember that when you make that woman feel like she is the best thing since sliced bread, she will do anything for you! If you uplift, enlighten and encourage her, even many of the problems that you now seek counseling for would become nonexistent.

I was coming down the stairs after a function several years ago and was walking beside a friend. There was a couple in front of us and the wife tripped and nearly fell. The husband said to her, "Honey, be careful." My friend said to me—and I thought the same—"Why didn't he just grab her arm and steady her?" Be careful? She could have been on the ground. It seemed like a "duh" moment! Just do the right thing. You are the man. Be what she needs.

We like to use the term *man up*. Well, a lot of Christian men need to man up! I want to see more men holding their wife's hand when they come to church. How about opening the car door for your wife? Can you just extend your hand to help her out of the car or down the steps? These ideas may seem simple, but what are you doing when you do these things? You are showing her—and others—that you love her as Christ loves the church. Christ died so that the church can become what she needs to be. If your wife feels so satisfied in her soul and treasured and valued in the knowledge that you give of yourself freely for her that her self-esteem rises, her self-confidence rises and her affection rises, she would reward you in ways that you long for.

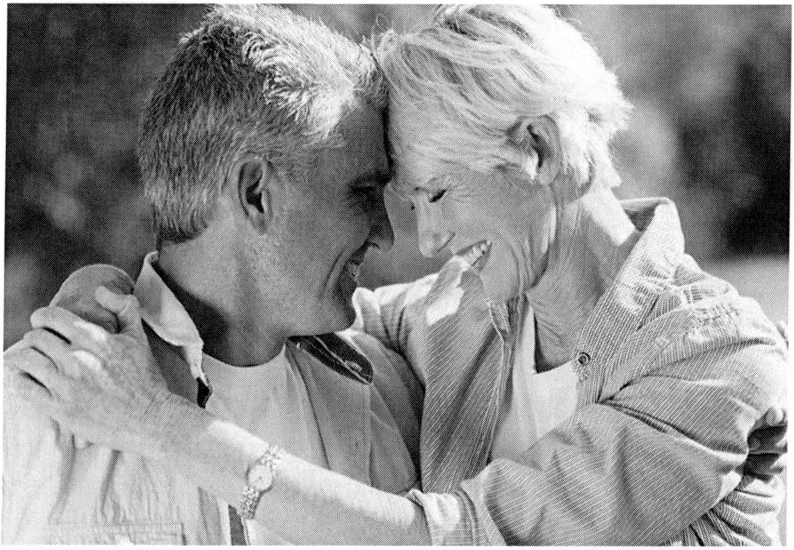

Chapter Seven

Understanding

Pastor Dave:

Information fuels positive transformation. Understanding how change happens and how the other person perceives things is important in knowing how best to relate to each other.

You cannot shout or nag positive changes in a person's life. Sometimes we would say such things as: "Why are you doing this again?" Then we would expect the person to change at that moment and never repeat the act. That, my friend, is not realistic. It is totally unrealistic to expect instant change. Change comes from several things. First, change comes through understanding. We have to first understand what makes a person act in a certain way. Once we gain an understanding, the next step is discussion. If the offended person does not know what has offended you, how can resolution come? The person has to be informed. Information is critical. Your discussion should be based on relevant information.

Here is an information nugget that will be of immense help in your relationship. The hardest person to change is someone else. Each of us has an idealized version of our husband or wife in our mind and we are all just itching to tell them what they need to do to become like that image; but it is hard to change someone else. The easiest person to change is yourself. So whenever changes need to be made, start with yourself first;

because if you want that person to change, there is probably something in you that needs to change to help bring about their change.

Change comes through recognition. Recognize that change is a process and, unfortunately, some changes will never materialize. You have to accept that you will never get 100 percent of what you want in this life. If you get 80 percent, rejoice. Now, if you get 20 percent, you're in trouble; you've got plenty of problems and plenty of work to do.

Change requires work. There is a dynamic in relationships that I call **triggers**. Now, what are triggers? Triggers are the things we do to a person that cause a specific response—usually negative—from that person. I had to learn my wife's triggers. And sometimes I learned the triggers the hard way. What I've realized over time is to begin to learn the things that trigger arguments, that trigger fights, that trigger unpleasant experiences. Let me give you an example. I am a person who likes to be on time and I have found that women have a challenge getting ready on time, even under the best circumstances. So, when it is time to go to church, I would start fussing with my wife. Perhaps I should not say "fussing"; let's just say we have an extended spirited discussion. We had a spirited discussion about why she is always late and cannot ever seem to get ready for church on time. She would coach me to "Take out your clothes the night before" and I never take out my clothes, yet I am always on time. She, on the other hand, prepares her clothes—irons them and ensures that everything is fixed—the night before. Then the next morning would come and she still would not be ready on time. And I would start arguing with her.

I realized that when I do that, she gets really upset. She does not appreciate me arguing with her because she is really trying to get ready. My scolding of her only makes her feel more overwhelmed. I have come to understand that women encounter diverse complications when they are trying to get dressed for an event. Sometimes the makeup isn't right, or the hairstyle isn't doing what it is supposed to do, or the dress does not fit like it did the last time and so they will try on dress after dress until they are satisfied...or give up. For me, if I take down a suit, I am wearing **that** suit. I do not care what is wrong with it. It seemed trivial to me, but I understand now that rowing her about how long she takes to get dressed is a trigger for her; so I have to be sensitive to that.

Here's what I do instead now. When it is time for my wife to get ready, I do everything I can to help her and then I leave her alone. I go downstairs to my computer and wait until she is ready. I do not argue or fight with her anymore because I realize that is not helpful. My time is better served doing something productive. Once I identified the trigger, then it became less of an issue. It is very important to identify triggers and find a solution rather than continuing to do the same thing and getting the same reaction each time.

Now, I used that simply as an example and I want to keep things in perspective and balance the picture. My wife is such a wonderful woman, she helps me select my clothes for church before she picks out her own. I think I can pick clothes, but she will come in and recommend something else that she thinks is better. And I respect her opinion. She'd choose a tie for me or she might say, "Well, I think this suit is better." She knows a lot about clothes, so she'd say, "For this occasion you need a darker suit." She will tell me certain things to help me in getting dressed. Once we've figure out everything, she would say, "Look, I do not want you to work on Sunday mornings because I know that you have to be ready to teach. So, whatever needs to be ironed, I'll iron it. Whatever needs to be ready, I'll present it to you and then you just put your clothes on." I want to make sure you know this when I talk about being annoyed by how long she takes to get ready. I appreciate what she does for me because it eliminates a lot of my headache and it takes a lot of pressure off me. Even when we travel, my wife says to me, without my asking, "Do not worry about ironing your clothes." I have never had to ask her to iron my clothes. I really appreciate that; it makes me feel special, so I try to do whatever she needs to feel special. We have a reciprocal relationship where we do things for each other because of our love and respect for one another. In every relationship, you have to figure out what helps you to achieve your objective so that it is not about who wins an argument but about what each person can do to make the relationship better.

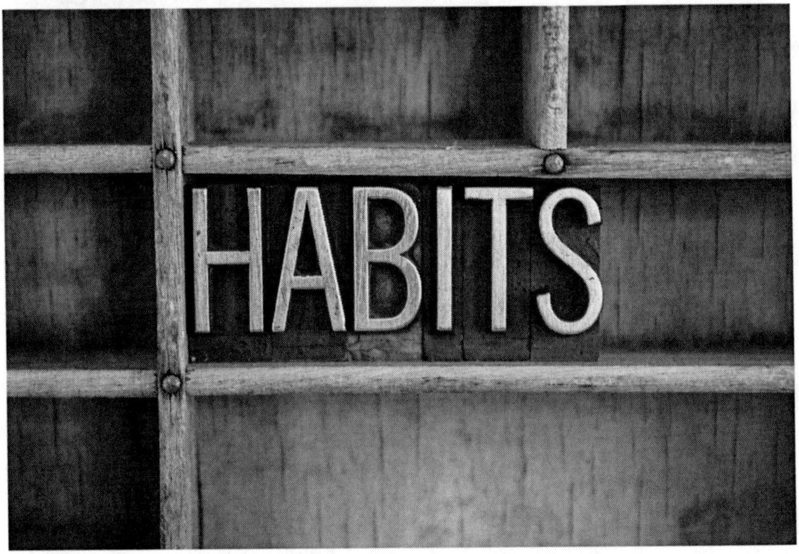
HABITS

Chapter Eight
Creating Good Habits

Habit 1. Romance

Pastor Angie:
WHILE WE ALL have issues in marriage and change is not easy, if each partner is dedicated to a better relationship, we can experience significant change and improvement in our quality of life. Just like in sports or with career goals, dedication and repetition can create new habits that become habits of desirable change. We know that developing new habits requires consistency. According to some behavioral scientists, it takes twenty-one days to form a habit. Let us break that goal down even smaller and start with seven days. Here is a challenge for our male readers: Say something nice to your wife every day for the next seven days. We will even give you some hints on how to do it. If you are bashful and do not want to say something to her in person, you can write your wife a note and put it in her purse, or in her medicine cabinet, or place it on the counter where she cooks or on the vanity where she fixes her makeup, or you can even put it in her shoe. Wouldn't that be a wonderful surprise, ladies? It is a wonderful thing for a woman to find a love note as she is putting on her shoes, or to find a rose on her pillow as she goes to sleep. It does not take

very much to brighten your wife's day. There are several small thoughtful gestures that make ladies feel very special.

PASTOR DAVE:

We recently had a marriage seminar, and one of the things that we concluded was that men need help when it comes to romance. Even now we have begun compiling a list of "romance recommendations" for men. The brothers need help, and there is no reason to be embarrassed about that. I am a brother that needs help too. I did not grow up in a very romantic environment. I grew up with people who went by names like Bobo, Shaft, Dirty Red and Sasquatch (my neighborhood friends from the streets) and we really were not into romance. As my life changed and I grew as a believer, I learned and grew in the area of romance. I had to develop new habits, because my old habits were not very productive. How did I re-educate myself? Sometimes I did not know what to do, until I discovered a great resource that I was not aware of in my own home—my children!

Here's an example of how I successfully enlisted their help a few years ago when my wife had gone away for three weeks. I wanted to make her feel special on her return but I was at a loss for what to do. I consulted with my kids and they gave me the most wonderful idea, something that I never would have thought of on my own. They told me to put flower petals on the floor and little envelopes with special messages—as well as money—in them, and all kinds of stuff. So I took their advice and set up a welcome that began with the petals. When my wife returned home, I blindfolded her and did not allow her to see anything until the time was right. I had the works! And that made me feel good. I took the blindfold off and led her to an envelope with money in it, which led to a bottle of cider, which led to a special gift. My wife was so surprised and pleased she exclaimed, "What happened to my husband!" She was overjoyed and my objective was achieved.

That experience showed me that I do not have to figure out everything on my own. That was one of the lessons I learned. Sometimes we need to learn, even if it is from our children or friends. You can get help with the areas you are not strong in and better the quality of your relationship. There is nothing as satisfying as seeing your wife overwhelmed by your romantic endeavors, especially when you know that you are not much of a romantic.

I am reminded even now that I need some more practice. An abbreviated version of our romance resource appears at the back of the book for husbands; only because it seems women do not have a problem with romance. Women seem to have it down to a tee.

HABIT 2. AVOIDING TRIGGERS

PASTOR DAVE:
Forming or reforming habits is work and a challenge; but we will always have challenges in relationships. The Apostle Paul warns that those who marry will face many troubles [or challenges] in this life (1 Corinthians 7:28 niv). This does not mean that those who are single do not face trouble or challenges. In other words, everybody faces trouble or challenges. Jesus put it this way: *In this world you shall have tribulation* (John 16:33). The conclusion? In this world you will have challenges. Since you are going to have challenges, what you want to know is how to overcome those challenges. Relationship challenges are mitigated by forming and establishing good habits; because your habits become your default behavior.

Someone once said: "All marriages are happy. It is the living together afterward that causes the problem." When you go through your marriage ceremony and you have all the flowers and the bubbles and everything, everybody is happy! The problem begins when you start living together. Another person said: "If love is blind, marriage can restore sight."

Let me give you another example about changing habits and behavior. I travel often and my wife travels often. Because I live very close to the airport, my philosophy is that when I come back home to The Bahamas, after I clear Customs, I should simply call home and announce that I've arrived, come and get me. That's normal for me. But I discovered that this does not work for my wife. I recognized that this behavior is a trigger and I need to change my habitual response and develop a new habit. Basically, what I learned is this: I would be at home watching a game or something like that and upon her return to the island, she would call and say, "I am at the airport." But she wouldn't say it in a nice tone, because in her mind I should have been at the airport waiting for her arrival. I didn't realize I should be at the airport because I think a little differently. I had to learn that being there for her as soon as she is ready is important to her. It was not important to me—but I do not live by myself; so I developed a new response that I practiced until it became a habit. Once it became a habit, it became my default behavior. So now I track her flights to ensure that I am aware of when she lands and I can be there for her. Marriage is not about what is important to one party; we have to recognize each other's needs and preferences and adapt for the sake of preserving a healthy marriage. Develop habits that make your marriage better.

PASTOR ANGIE:
The only person I like to wait on is the Lord.

I would like to make a very important, even critical, point here. What each of us has to do is focus on learning to modify our behavior, because it is almost impossible to modify your personality. No matter what kind of personality you have, it is difficult to modify that because, according to psychologists, personality is formed in the first four years of life. Whatever you are going to be like in terms of your personality is already formed at a very early age and does not really change; personality is very difficult to modify. The thing that you can modify is how you behave on a daily basis, particularly in light of how your behavior affects someone else.

We cannot stress enough the value of repetition in developing or modifying habits. Consistency is essential. Why do I say that? Sometimes you do not get it the first time. Sometimes you do not get it the second time. For those of us who are a little slow, we do not get it the fifty-fifth time. But you have to keep the goal in mind and you have to keep taking action that gets you closer to your destiny. Do not expect instant results; keep working, practicing and repeating the favorable behavior until it is incorporated into your daily routine as a good habit.

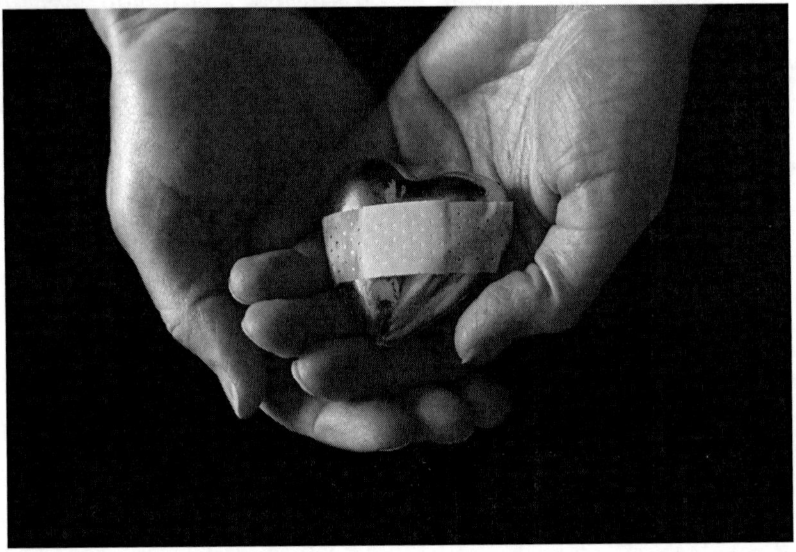

Chapter Nine

FORGIVENESS

PASTOR DAVE:

NOW HERE'S THE next key in successful relationships: forgiveness. Forgiveness is one of the most important keys in a relationship, in a marriage relationship, or any kind of relationship. This key is so important that Jesus talked about it repeatedly. His principle was: *When you stand praying, if you hold anything against anyone, forgive them* (Mark 11:2 niv). We should understand from His statement that forgiveness is essential to healthy relationships. You have to be able to forgive, even when you feel like you are right. Forgiveness is a requirement whether you feel like it or not. One of my greatest accomplishments in life is learning to forgive on a regular basis and making it a part of my existence. Because of the way I grew up and the way I acted early in my life, I didn't forgive a lot of people. In fact, if you did something to me, I'd want to assault you, or run behind you with a weapon, or burn down your house; these were the thoughts that would go through my mind. I was not the forgiving type; I had to learn forgiveness. There are some other people out there who had the same kind of problem I had, I am sure. I am going to make a comment about forgiveness and then I am going to ask my wife to make a comment because she is an expert in forgiveness. She knows how to forgive and she knows how to encourage me to be forgiving as well.

Colossians 3:12-13 says: *Therefore, as the elect of God, holy and beloved, put on tender mercies, kindness, humility, meekness, longsuffering; bearing with one another.* I want to focus on the last three words, bearing with one another. Sometimes you have to bear with one another. Sometimes you have to look at people's faults, their mistakes, the things that they do wrong, and say: "You know what? I am going to cut you some slack because I am human just like you and I did some of those same things." When you do not bear with people, you make it seem as if you do not go through the same things they do. But, when you bear with others, you show them that you understand and appreciate better what they are experiencing. All of us have shortcomings. In the same way, as the Bible says, that you will have trouble in this world, you also will have shortcomings, and you will make mistakes—sometimes big mistakes. In fact, God knew you were going to make mistakes, and that's why He said if you sin, He is faithful and just to forgive you. God will forgive your mistakes; so you have to forgive the mistakes of others.

Now, forgiveness is not a license to keep doing the same things. But forgiveness is a necessary part of bearing with one another. Colossians 3:13 continues: *and forgiving one another, if anyone has a complaint against another; even as Christ forgave you, so you also must do.* We have to forgive.

PASTOR ANGIE:
Amen. I think one of the problems in marriage, Pastor Dave, is that a lot of people operate in a spirit of un-forgiveness. A lot of people have marital problems that stem from un-forgiveness. If we traced the origins of our problems, we may find that a lot of us believers have un-forgiveness toward even our parents. Some of us came up at a time when we couldn't express to our parents our displeasure over things they did; and a lot of us internalized our pain. And even though we are

Forgiveness

born again, we walk around with the spirit of un-forgiveness operating in us. I am not saying that some of the things that were done to you, to me, to all of us, were not really bad, or in some cases treacherous. But the Word of God says that when we go before the Father, we must forgive. Jesus said that when we go to present our gifts, before we present them we are supposed to go and forgive. Some of us, I dare say, are withholding forgiveness from someone. Maybe we know someone we've offended; we might not think that we were wrong but we must make sure we clear the air. If you operate as a person who is full of un-forgiveness, that spirit will be exacerbated in marriage. The opportunities for un-forgiveness will be heightened because you are now in close proximity of this person.

People of God, we are not trying to trivialize forgiveness. We know some of you have been raped, you've been molested, your spouse may have even spent money from your joint account that you were saving for some important cause. Nevertheless, you have to release that situation to the Lord. You have to release your spouse, you have to release your sister, you have to release your ex-husband, and you have to release your ex-wife, your ex-girlfriend, your ex-boyfriend, or your father.

I carried a lot of acrimony in me but didn't realize it. I was a very forgiving person; I forgave everyone. I find it easy to forgive; I do not hold a grudge. I would say what I have to say then I am finished with that. Next? Let's move on: What do you need from me? So I do not hold un-forgiveness…or so I thought. I had a lot of negative things done to me even as a believer, even by Christian people. I used to say we cannot have the same Father and someone would do something like that to me. But you know something? I am human and I probably did something to someone that they considered offensive. We are human; we are not divine.

Several years ago, something occurred that changed my life. I had been saved for quite a few years then. I was asleep one night and I was attacked in my sleep because a door was open that I did not realize was open. If you have un-forgiveness in your life, you have an open door; it's an open door to the enemy. As loving as I was to everybody else, I had an open door and the door was un-forgiveness. Who did I not forgive? I did not forgive my natural father. I talk about my father and my daddy. My daddy is the man who raised me; he is a very good man. But my natural father is another story. I didn't know I had un-forgiveness for him and that this opened a door for me to be attacked. That night it was an evil spirit; and I had to pray through. Pastor Dave and my cousin got on the phone and together they had a prayer chain for me. I didn't realize I had un-forgiveness in my life even though I would say things like this: "How could a man be so educated, be so smart, sit down to eat and not know if your child has eaten?" And I would have these conversations with myself, not with anyone else. What I should have done was use the Word of God to capture those thoughts to the obedience of Christ and cleanse my heart. I should have used the Word of God and not my feelings. I do not care how much hype we get into, the Word of God—not our feelings—must be the foundation of our thoughts. And I should have been grateful and said, "Lord, I thank you that my natural father didn't do the things for me that a father should but God, you provided for me, I never lacked." I had nice clothes, I had food, I had shelter and I had a stepfather who cared for me more than my father. So I should have counted my blessings and not be ungrateful. I should have released the pain; I should have said it hurts but I release it because God has been good to me. Un-forgiveness is a poison. My husband said to me once: "Un-forgiveness is like drinking poison and expecting the other person to die." (Actually, the original quote came from Nelson Mandela.)

Colossians 3:12 says, *Therefore as God is the elective God, Holy and beloved, put on tender mercies; kindness, humility, meekness, long-suffering, bearing with one another.* The first time I told my husband the story of my father he told me, "We should go spit on his grave." I waited a long time to tell him that story because my husband loves me very much and I knew he would be angry about it. Because he loves me very much he was offended that someone did this to me. There are some things you may not even want to tell your spouse, if it is going cause them to be offended on your behalf.

PASTOR DAVE:
Yes, I remember when my wife first told me her story. I said, "We need to go spit on his grave." I could not believe that her father never did a thing for her in her entire life. To me that was unbelievable. I was saved at the time, but that was my initial reaction. Forgiveness was not something that came easy for me. I did eventually repent of the thought.

PASTOR ANGIE:
His reaction is one of the reasons I didn't tell him that story for a long time. I knew I had to use wisdom in dealing with my situation. If you are dealing with your spouse and you know they feel a certain way, you have to be careful about what you say and what you reveal to them. Christian people say things sometimes that they have to ask forgiveness for; so I made sure I said to Dave, "Did you hear what you just said?" Later, someone in my church told me that they had told their children to go spit on their daddy's grave and I rebuked her. I said, "In the name of Jesus, you're wrong." (But I didn't tell her my story.) She chose that man for her children and it didn't work out somehow, but she does not have any right to go and spit on someone's grave; that shows she's harboring un-forgiveness.

We have to learn to forgive each other, even when we have been hurt. Forgiveness is beneficial to our relationship and marriage. Although it may be painful, sometimes in the end it is for the greater good that we forgive.

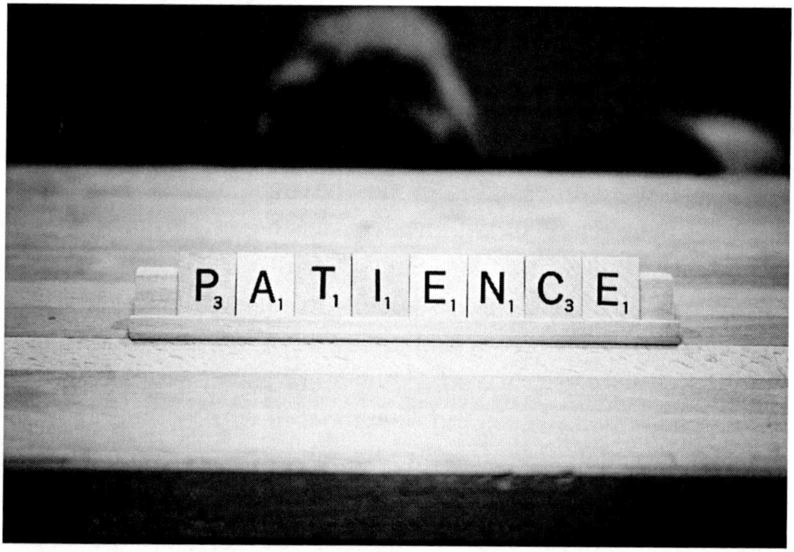
PATIENCE

Chapter Ten

PATIENCE

PASTOR DAVE:
FORGIVENESS TIES IN closely to our next key to marriage success: patience. The first book of Corinthians states that love is patient. You can tell if love is in you by how patient you are with others. Sometimes having patience is a really difficult challenge. Oftentimes you want to see instant changes in others, but the hardest person in the world to change is someone else. The easiest person in the world to change is yourself. We should be patient with others because God is patient with us. He is working on all of us, so we should work with each other. We should remember to work with each other not on each other. We need to be supportive and encouraging and allow each other the room to grow. Sometimes we have to give a hint; sometimes we have to give a suggestion; sometimes we have to let the person make the same mistake twenty-five times and, as they make the mistake, instead of condemning them, just remind them that they made the same mistake again and we'd really appreciate if they did this differently. Our language, when addressing issues, is so important; because when we are not expressing ourselves with love and kindness, we are not fulfilling the law of God. God says love is patient; so if you say you are walking in love, you have to be patient.

It is not easy to be patient. Bahamians have a well-known expression: we say we are "short of patience." Well, you have

Patience

to increase your patience level because God said that love is patient and you are in Him. And if you are in Him then your patience level needs to increase. An important key to remember when it comes to patience is that progress is more important than perfection. You have to acknowledge progress. Your spouse may have done something wrong and the two of you may have discussed it previously but the situation hasn't turned around as quickly as you would like. (In fact, sometimes it may never turn around.) However, if your spouse is moving in the right direction, —even if they are making small steps— you have to recognize progress, because progress is more important that perfection. Perfection is very difficult to attain and if you criticize someone who is genuinely trying, they are going to get discouraged and probably give up. So patience is an absolute virtue in every relationship.

When we think about patience, we have to consider the value of our relationships. How important is this marriage to you? When I look at my marriage, I thank God for a good wife; and since I have a good wife, why would I not be patient with her? You need to be patient with one another because you realize the value of your relationship.

One of the things I can say is that my life got better when I entered into marriage with my wife. My life has continually gone up on the scale because of our relationship. But if there is something that goes wrong, I need to be patient because I see where I am going. If I am offended and I take that offense and lose my patience over that offense, I am damaging a very valuable relationship. I am concluding before the conclusion has concluded. We have to be very patient with each other.

PASTOR ANGIE:
I had to learn patience too. Clearly, it goes back to the Word. If we all lived the Word, things would be okay. It really does not matter what my personal feelings are, I have to live the Word

of God. Many of us put the Word into practice in most areas of our life but we do not put the Word into practice with our spouse. Here's an example of what we do: We come to church and we act all lovey-dovey in public but live a completely different scenario at home. What really matters is what happens in private. A lot of us are kinder to people outside our home than we are to our spouse. I should be kindest to my spouse, then to my children and parents, and then to everyone else.

Apostle Paul reminds us that love is kind, it is patient; love always believes, love perseveres (1 Corinthians 13). We must endure some things. I look like my mother but I have a lot of my natural father's family's traits. His baby sister, my aunt, is still alive—she is ninety-one years old—and that woman does not play. I remember when I was in my early twenties, I made a comment and my mother said to me, "For God's sake! You are just like your Aunty So-and-So." And I responded, "For real?" I realized her DNA was inside me, meaning, I was bold and candid like her; I never felt the need to tiptoe around anyone. Aunty So-and-So at ninety-one still "isn't ever scared" and I have decided that I like that; I will take that trait. But I realize the trait is already ingrained in who I am.

In the Christian community we say "you got to find some spirit, some ancestral spirits." Because I know I have the tendency to shoot off my mouth, I decided to go in the completely opposite direction, sometimes even letting people take advantage of me. I could really damage them because of some of the things I know about them. These people may have thought I was being foolish by being silent, but I was not. I was killing that spirit of anger and pride by teaching myself that I do not need to answer someone without my speech being seasoned with salt, as the Word says. So that part of me I had to put not at the foot of the cross but in the grave; I had to bury it.

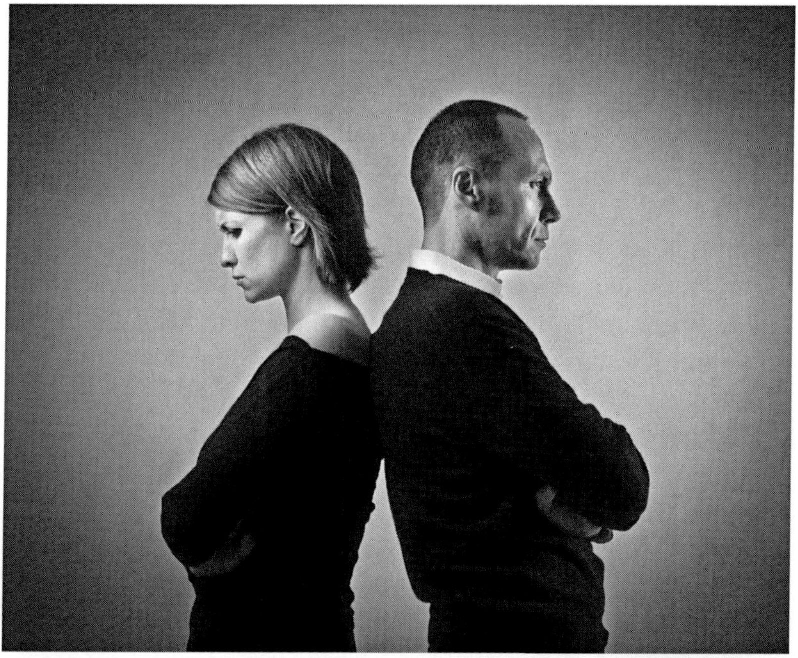

Chapter Eleven

ANGER

PASTOR DAVE:

THAT LEADS US to our next point: anger. The truth of the matter is that anger is a human emotion that we all have to deal with. Like every emotion, it was given to us by God for a purpose. Anger is not bad in and of itself; it simply serves as a tool to spur us on in a necessary course of action. The Bible actually talks about anger and tells us how we ought to handle it. What I appreciate about God is that He tells us what the problems are ahead of time and how to deal with them long before we have even encountered them. We should simply look to His guidelines, since He is the designer. If He designed us, then He has the solution for us. Here is what God says about managing anger: *Be angry and do not sin* (Ephesians 4:26). Now, when you get angry, it is easy to sin because anger produces a violent reaction; sometimes you feel like throwing missiles and doing all kinds of stuff. But God is saying that it is okay to get angry because anger is a human response to negative circumstances or to something that disturbs you. It is okay to be angry, but you must be careful to manage those feelings properly; because your anger can cause you to do things that can destroy the good parts of your relationship. Therefore I can be angry at my wife, but if I hit her with something, it would be counterproductive to our marriage (and given her personality she'd probably hit me back and the war would begin with no good ending in sight).

PASTOR ANGIE:
You're probably right, I would hit you back.

PASTOR DAVE:
Then I would do something that would cause me to end up in jail and our marriage to terminate. Satisfying your impulse to react in anger does not produce a favorable end.

PASTOR ANGIE:
You wouldn't go to jail; I wouldn't call the police. But we would have lost something valuable. But listen: We do not hit one another. Take it out of your mind.

PASTOR DAVE:
The Bible advises us: *"Be angry, and do not sin": do not let the sun go down on your wrath, nor give place to the devil* (Ephesians 4:26-27). There is an anger that you can rightfully experience and there is an anger you can hold onto that gives place to the devil. Processing your anger in a way that does not give place to the devil happens when you recognize what you are angry about and you seek a **resolution instead of retribution.** Remember that your focus should be resolution not retribution. whenever you are angry remind yourself to repeat "resolution not retribution." When you are angry, many times your immediate desire is for retribution; you would like to pay the person back for their offense against you. But we have to understand that whenever we are angry it is because something went wrong and we need to focus on the issue instead of the person who caused the issue. That's why the Bible says do not give place to the devil.

In our early stages of marriage, I found it difficult to find resolutions because I grew up totally retribution oriented.

Keys to Marriage and Relationship Success

If someone offended me, I would physically harm them or verbally insult them. As time went on, I got better; and my wife really helped me with this because she was able to talk about what offended her and then make the decision to move on. She was great with that because she would look for a resolution after her initial reaction. I had to learn that over a period of time and the process is still going on. I am much better than I used to be but I am not perfect with it. In fact, I am doing very well according to my standards; I am doing excellently.

PASTOR ANGIE:
You're doing well. You're doing very well!

PASTOR DAVE:
Sometimes, instead of seeking resolution, we simply seek to confirm our anger. When a person has done something wrong to us we respond, "See what you did!" and we begin to explain to them how they have failed, as if they do not realize what they have done. In such cases, all we have done is successfully blamed them; we have not brought about a resolution. Blaming does not accomplish a resolution. When you have conflict, you have to stop and decide: "How do I make this situation not recur?" and "How do I make it better in the current environment?" After practicing this approach consistently, I began to understand that it is possible to resolve differences; I just have to seek solutions as opposed to maintaining anger.

Another practice that is very important is to make sure you have the facts before you draw a conclusion. People would say things to me or report to me something that someone said and I would not believe them. Do you know why? I need to establish the truth of what they are saying for myself before I react to it. I've discovered through my relationships that you can act on something that somebody told you and then find out later it was wrong.

PASTOR ANGIE:

Let me just say something about that. That is wrong and it is also very dangerous when you make statements or inferences based upon incomplete or wrong information. There are a lot of relationships that have been destroyed because somebody carried partial stories. Even worse, some people tell things that are entirely untrue out of malicious intent. By not getting the full story you have a false report that may cause you to respond in a way that embarrasses yourself. There are people whose assignment is straight from hell to keep people separated. Someone may come to you and say, "Pastor Dave, you know what I heard, Pastor Joseph does not really like you." That report was hatched in hell: Pastor Joseph didn't say that; he may have had a question about something you are doing. So let's not use our tongues for false or misleading stories. As believers, use your spiritual authority and respond with: "I know you're concerned; let's go and confront this person together." In this way you are following the Word. The Bible says you are to talk to the person who has wronged you and if they will not believe you, then return with a witness. In the presence of two or three witnesses let the word be established, and then gossip would cease.

You also have to be careful about what you hear your spouse say, and seek clarification; because sometimes we hear incorrectly or we misinterpret what we hear. That's why we should always ask questions and be very slow in passing judgment. In addition to that, we should deal with issues quickly. Sometimes we allow things to fester for a long time. It is best to deal with troublesome matters quickly. If you cannot deal with the issue on your own, find a counselor.

PASTOR DAVE:

And here's another important aspect of dealing with anger. Separate the person from the behavior when expressing your anger. What do I mean? This is what we sometimes do: We say, "You are stupid," when we mean, "You engaged in stupid behavior." Actually, you should not use the word *stupid* because it is a very derogatory word. You should find a more appropriate way of expressing your feelings. For example, you can say, "You didn't use your best judgment" or "You erred in this instance." Yes, sometimes you have to come up with fancy terminology to avoid insulting someone. Because "you are stupid" are fighting words.

Another important point is to avoid using the word *always;* because in most instances the behavior happens occasionally or the person says what they do occasionally, not always. When we become angry, we tend to use absolutes. Using absolute terms closes the doors to resolution. It is better to say: "I do not like it when you say that or when you behave in that manner."

PASTOR ANGIE:

As a believer, a born-again Kingdom citizen, remember that the onus or responsibility is on you to do what the Word says. As far as it rests with you, live at peace with all men. Let me tell you who all men includes. All men includes your parents. All men includes your children. And all men includes your siblings. I have found in my years of counseling that there are Christians who do not speak to their siblings. After reading this chapter, please make sure you are not one of those persons. Yes, your parents died and your siblings took all the property and didn't give you what you should have been given. But think about the problem this way: You can live in only one house at a time. It is not worth it to ruin the relationship with your brother or sister. Whatever you have, thank God for it.

Anger

And if you need a house, God will bless you. Live at peace with all men.

PASTOR DAVE:
The Bible does say that love covers a multitude of sins. What I want you to remember is that verbal abuse sparks anger and wounds those who are precious to you; so learn how not to be verbally abusive. Learn how to use alternative language, as I mentioned earlier. The language that you use can inflame a situation, so it is very important to understand that you have to use appropriate language. Always ask questions or make statements that are not all-inclusive. Do not say: "You always...", but rather, "You have done this a number of times...." Also, if your spouse has demonstrated improvements, then you have to mention that too. You have to keep your complaint in perspective. Remember this: Your spouse is not your adversary. Sometimes couples end up in adversarial relationships and are always arguing and fighting. You have to come to the realization that you want to have a good destiny with your marriage partner. And you do not want your destiny to be complicated. So if you do not want it to be complicated, you have to act in a way that simplifies things.

I want to tell you a quick story about how to eliminate anger. It is a funny story. A lady and her husband went to a therapist because they had a problem with constant fighting. The therapist began by asking them what the problem was. The wife had a long list of problems that were about the husband. The therapist asked the husband to comment on what the wife was saying but he responded no comment. The therapist went into a little bit more detail with the couple and started to analyze their problem. After a while he announced, "You know, I found a solution." The wife said, "Okay. This problem has been plaguing me so long, tell me what the solution is." He said, "I have used this solution in other circumstances. I am going to go and get my special formula." So he got this bottle—a specially colored bottle—called 'The Formula,' brought it to her and said, "Now, what I want you to do is, when your husband does the things he is always doing, drink a little bit of this formula and then swish it around in your mouth until the problem goes away." She came back a week later and said, "You know, Doc, that formula is amazing! What is in that bottle?" The therapist answered, "It is water."

Sometimes we have to realize that our solutions are simpler than we think and focus on solutions. As I discussed earlier, if you have successfully ascribed blame and established who was wrong, you have done nothing to solve your dilemma. Try to remember that you are in this together.

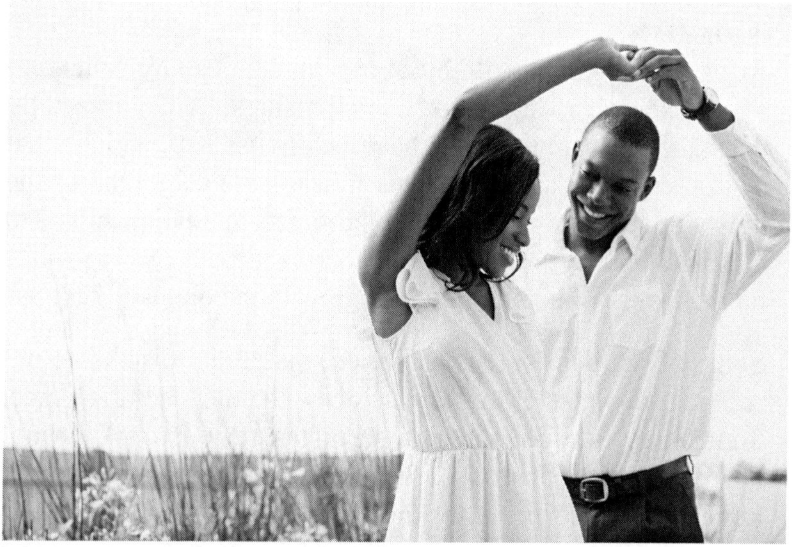

Chapter Twelve

Boundaries

Pastor Dave:
Now, let's talk a little bit about boundaries. We're talking about keys to successful relationships, and especially marriage; so, naturally, we have to discuss some things that can potentially cause problems in a relationship. One of the most important keys in avoiding problems in relationships is to establish boundaries. These boundaries include placing limits on the level of interaction you have with the opposite sex.

Some of us, when we get married, make the mistake of not recognizing that the way we interact with others has to change. Sometimes certain behaviors seem innocent, but we do not understand the potential damage they can cause. You should build barriers to prevent other people from damaging your relationship. Before you got married, you may have been in a relationship with or had a friend of the opposite sex. After you got married, you continue with this relationship: they continue to call you, or you continue to call them, and talk in an innocent manner; you may even go out with the person for a casual outing. And because this is a longtime friend, and you may wonder why your husband or your wife is offended. Even if you are not married but are in a girlfriend/boyfriend relationship, you may wonder why that person is so upset. Well, they have a reason to be offended: open doors can make your relationship vulnerable to attack. Oftentimes you may not have any evil intention and the other person may not have evil intention, but there is one who has evil intention, who will figure out a way to make it evil. So you have to protect yourself. I made some mistakes early on in my marriage in terms of establishing proper boundaries. My wife and I had to work together to create an understanding that we considered reasonable and acceptable to both sides. Let me clarify that the mistakes I made and later corrected in terms of opposite-sex relationships did not cause me to have extramarital affairs or anything like that. I have never been in an affair. I have been 100 percent faithful to my wife. In the early years of marriage I had a friend of the opposite sex who would ask me to go places and do things. I didn't tell my wife about this and she found out through one of her friends; a friend, I guess, who was concerned after she saw the friend and me riding together. She was a good friend, but the situation did not look good.

When those kinds of situations happen, you feel like rolling up on the news-carrying person and straightening things out, right? In order to prevent conflict, you need to establish boundaries. Here are the boundaries we have established. We do not get into conversations with the opposite sex or have interactions with the opposite sex unless we have the other's approval. If I say I am going to talk to this person or that person, or I am going to see that person, I do so with approval only. We make sure that the boundaries are what we are both comfortable with. Sometimes you have to meet regarding business matters and it may require being seen publicly with someone of the opposite sex. Make sure your spouse knows and approves of the interactions.

PASTOR ANGIE:
I want to stress that that advice is good not only for friends of the opposite sex. As a woman, you may have a girlfriend, a really nice girlfriend, to whom you may have attached yourself

too quickly. As a man you may have a male friend with whom you're too close. Some people, even though they are grown men or women, are so attached to their friends that you never see them alone. It is always Bonnie and Betty; always two people, two females or two males. You need friends, but there are some things you do not discuss with friends. There are some private things and some emotions that are only for your spouse. Ladies, you may find yourself telling your girlfriend more than you tell your husband. This is not good. Your girlfriend may start to give you advice, and, if she is single or divorced or in a bad marriage, her attitude might pollute the advice she gives. Maybe she is in a good marriage; even so, she may be giving you advice that is not from the Throne of God. So watch your attachments. Period.

Pastor Dave:

That leads us to our next point. Never discuss the faults of your spouse with the opposite sex or a friend. Sometimes there are things you need to resolve privately; those things do not need to be a community issue. Sometimes when you have friends, be they of the opposite sex or one of "your boys" or "your girls," you can find yourself talking about your spouse. Never do that. The only conversation you should have when you are talking about your spouse's faults is with a counselor; you should not be talking with a friend. There are some things that are best kept private and best dealt with on a professional level. And, men, when you share these things, especially with the opposite sex, with the secretary—or the sex-etary, or whatever you call her—she will start figuring out how to fix your problems; and as she starts solving the problems that your wife didn't solve, you then start to defer to her—your secretary. That's why so many relationships have gone awry. You have to establish boundaries, because boundaries protect you.

PASTOR ANGIE:
One other thing. Whether your children are young children or adult children, you are not to divulge their business. It really used to hurt my heart when I would hear people talk ill about their children. You should not talk negatively about your children, even with another relative. You're supposed to go to your children and talk to them; and you're supposed to pray for them. The fact that one of your children did something negative is not news for the whole family chat; that's not right. It's not right for you as a parent to divulge your children's business.

Here are some more important boundaries. Do not allow members of the opposite sex to come to your house if your spouse is not there. That's a simple boundary but it is an important boundary. Not that you're scared of yourself; you're just protecting your marriage. Besides, you have neighbors. There was a time my husband was away and I had to have a repairman come to the house to fix some things and he came after hours. After he had completed his work, he wanted to sit down. The television was on. Now, I am the kind of person who, if I want to have a sleep, I just turn on the TV; I never make it through a movie. So I said to myself that if I sit down with this man with this TV on, I could see myself falling asleep in this house. My daughter was in college, my son does not live at the house, and my husband was away. You get the picture. So I said to the gentleman, "No, you cannot take a seat. I am sorry, but you have to leave now; I have to go to bed," and I promptly escorted him out, though I was gracious. There are some things you just do not do. You just do not do.

PASTOR DAVE:
The situation Pastor Angie described above had to have been an emergency; because if it is not an emergency, the repairman can come when more than one person is at home. It is important

to establish those boundaries—common sense boundaries—that protect your marriage from simple but potentially harmful situations.

PASTOR ANGIE:

We do not need to be stereotypical, in the sense that we do not need to have our marriages going awry. Jesus said He came that we might have life and have it more abundantly (John 10:10). Abundant life isn't just money; it includes abundance in relationships, interpersonal relationships with my brothers and sisters in Christ, with my family, with my children, and with my spouse.

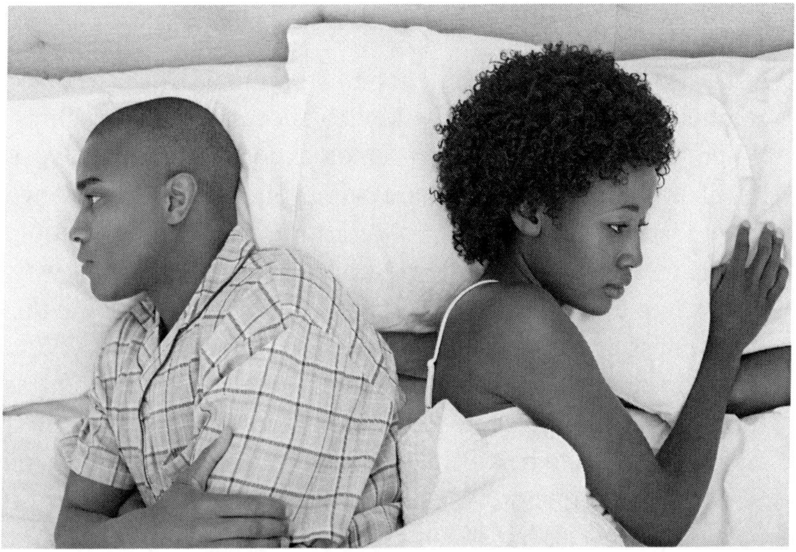

Chapter 13

Communication

Pastor Dave:

Let's talk a little bit about communication because communication is really *the* key to successful relationships. When you have effective communication, you can solve a lot of problems. Let me share with you some keys that we have discovered in terms of constructive communication. Sometimes you can say the right thing but in the wrong way. For example, you say to your spouse: "Why are you doing this foolishness again?" instead of saying, "Honey, I need you to work on this." The second statement has the same intent as the first but it is presented differently. You always want your communication to be affirmative. You want to say: "I need you to do this better," not "Why you always doin' this wrong?" It is a simple tweak but it can make a world of difference. The Bible says a soft answer turns away wrath. So if you answer harshly or if you communicate harshly, you cause a harsh reaction. You want a response and not a reaction.

Pastor Angie:

You want to communicate in a way that builds trust and strengthens the relationship. When you're married and you are communicating with members of the opposite sex, one of the most important things for you to do is to understand how to compliment appropriately. You may say something like: "You are looking good today." That's not the right way to say it. You should say: "That outfit looks nice on you." Or go even further by not saying "on you"; simply say: "That is a nice outfit." Men, be aware that sometimes paying a compliment to a woman who is deprived of compliments may illicit a greater reaction than you were hoping for. She may think: "Oh! He said I look good," or, "Oh, wow, he likes me." When all you were doing was telling her the outfit was nice. The same goes for men. Sometimes paying a well-meaning compliment to a man can be a stroke to his ego and cause him to misinterpret your intentions.

Always keep lines of communication open. One of the things that we can do in relationships is create roadblocks to communication. You always want to make sure that you are accessible. Sometimes we get angry and we retreat into silence or we create roadblocks to communication. Keep the lines of communication open, because when you are silent you cause imaginations to flourish. Your spouse can start imagining scenarios or coming up with their own conclusions. So long as you are communicating, your spouse is hearing what is on your mind; but when you go silent, they have to wonder what you are thinking or what you are about to do.

Understand your spouse's nonverbal communication. Sometimes you have to study a person so that when you see certain behaviors, you know something is wrong. It is important to identify the nonverbal signals. A spouse who stands and fold their arms and then contorts their face may be saying: "I am irritated", or "I am closed off." You have to understand your spouse's nonverbal communication. Now, it takes some research sometimes but it is important for us to study each other; because when we study each other we know better how to respond to each other. If you learn the language of nonverbal communication, you can pick up signals even before a word is spoken; and that's so important when it comes to communication.

The next thing to do is to ask questions. One of the most important questions to ask is: "Do you understand what I said?" It is also a good idea to follow up and ask your spouse to repeat what they heard. They may answer yes, they understood what you *said;* but in repeating what they *heard,* you realize they understood something completely different from what you said or thought you had communicated. So have the person repeat what is being communicated so that you are assured that they understood what you said. Understand the silent cries (internal pain that is now outwardly expressed) those things that are irritating to you when you do not know it outwardly.

Pastor Dave:

Now we get to the spiritual communication and connection. This is one of the most important aspects of a relationship. The persons who are not part of our Kingdom—the Kingdom of God—and do not share our philosophy, will ignore this part of relationships. But this has been the most important part of relationships for me. We have to pray for one another; we have to understand that we are three-part beings—spirit, soul, and body. We cannot just deal with two parts; we have to deal with all three. Actually, the spirit part of us causes everything else to work right. I have found in my life that when I get my spiritual life together, this impacts the other aspects of my life. That is why my wife and I get together and we pray for one another on a regular basis. If my wife has an issue, she will come to me and we pray. Even if there is no issue, sometimes we wake up in the morning and we just pray together. We pray individually, we pray for each other, and we pray together.

PASTOR ANGIE:
It is good to give your spouse time to pray alone. Sometimes Pastor Dave says his first prayer in the morning by himself, and that's fine, because he needs to talk to God as an individual. The most important relationship is the relationship with the Lord.

Do not put yourself in the place of God. Make sure as a wife you know your place: God is first. Husbands, let your wife love God more than she loves you; do not become an idol. Do not become her idol. God is a jealous God. So let the man go and pray; let the lady go and pray. The two of you can talk to each other later.

You have to make room for the Holy Spirit in your relationships; and you do that by practicing righteous living. You want to be aligned with the Holy Spirit. You want to be living according to the principles of God. You want to be praying. You want to have a spiritual life that includes praise and worship, prayer and meditation. When you do these things, you are able to live a righteous life. You live a righteous life by meditating on His Word and internalizing it. That's what the Bible says. Therefore we have to continually keep the Word in our relationship.

Intercede for your spouse when you are not together. Before we were married, one night I was in Oklahoma and as I was having my devotions, I saw a spiritual attack. I didn't understand in those days what that was, but I knew it was time to pray. There are times you pray as usual and there are times you go into intense prayer for your spouse. Even if your spouse is not acting right, you pray, because you see the spirit that wants to attack your spouse. As a wife, you are supposed to be your husband's chief intercessor. You're supposed to be the spiritual security in your home. Likewise, he's supposed to be your chief intercessor. You pray, because the devil is getting Christians to move the boundaries and to miscommunicate. But the Holy Spirit showed me that the devil does not move a boundary quickly; he moves it a little at a time. He moves it just a bit and then he stops and waits for our reaction. He moves a boundary slowly so we do not see what is happening to us mentally, socially, and spiritually. He dulling our spiritual senses. And when our spiritual senses are dulled we do not heed the Word of God for our marriage. Instead, we heed the stuff we see on TV and unwittingly accept the spirit of the world. We must constantly be in a place with God where we can hear and recognize what is happening in our marriage.

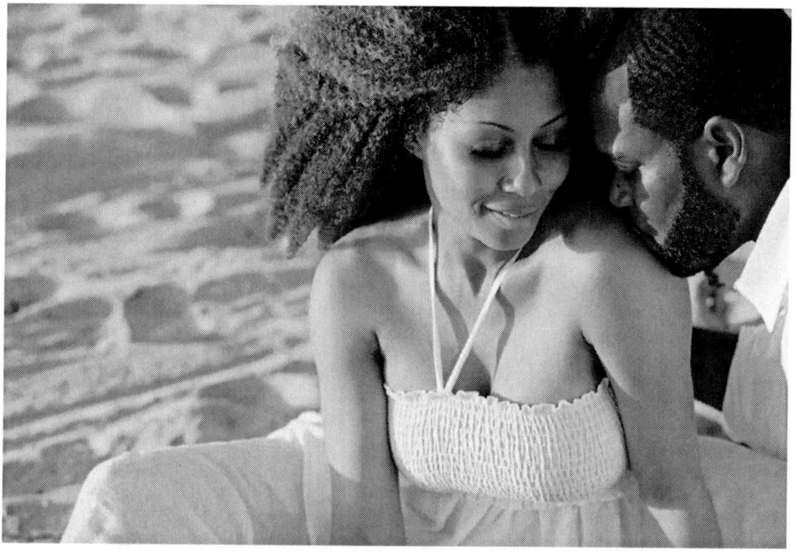

Chapter 14

Sex and Marriage

Pastor Angie:

I WOULD LIKE to move to a very important subject. It is said that the two things that are most likely to destroy a marriage are sex and money. Before we talk about sex in marriage, let me say something that the Holy Spirit told me to say. He is tired of the people of God fornicating. It is a problem in the Body of Christ. I repeat: Fornication is a problem in the Body of Christ. Fornication causes problems to transfer to marriage; read 1 Corinthians 7. If you had only one partner that would be perfect, and we know we do not live in a perfect world; but the Word of God remains true: You must not fornicate. You must stop fornicating as a believer. Pastor Dave gave me permission to share what follows. The Holy Spirit said to me that as married people, some of us have been poor examples in our homes; therefore our children have decided that they do not want to be married, but they want to have sex because they want to have certain feelings. We as parents must take authority and we must stand on the Word of God no matter what. Whatever adult children do is what they will do; but we must have a standard in our homes that fornication is still wrong and adultery is still wrong.

We have been lulled asleep spiritually. We say churches have no power, but there is also no power in the pew. People come to church for a fix; but we do not want to fix ourselves. If we fix ourselves, we'd have better marriages, because the Holy Spirit would enlighten us even to the things we do not see. I believe and know that God is upset by how we are living in the church. God is not pleased that we could come to church and yet live lives that disobey his commands—not suggestions—when it comes to sexual activity. An intimate relationship means that you cannot be intimate with someone else; or if you become intimate with someone else, you feel guilty about it to the point where it bothers you and you are uncomfortable: that's called having a conscience. But if you can come to church every week and continue to fornicate, that means you are in a backslidden state. The good thing is that God says He is married to the backslider (Jeremiah 3:14). But you cannot keep sinning and disobeying God without being utterly and completely destroyed.

PASTOR DAVE:
Now let's talk about sex in marriage. I am going to speak to the men.

I have found over and again that men in the church and outside the church, but particularly in the church, are having a difficult time when it comes to sex. The difficulty is largely because men and women lack an understanding of how the other is designed physiologically, emotionally and psychologically. What do I mean? Men often are under the impression that women think the way they do sexually, and women are under the same impression about men. Men and women are VERY, VERY different sexually. Men have a predominant hormone called testosterone and it makes a man sexually aggressive. Women often do not realize this, so they think something is wrong when the man wants sex often. Men have an incredible sex drive. Women, on the other hand, have a hormone called estrogen that makes them react differently to men. Men are stimulated by sight: all they need to see is something exposed on a woman and they go off like a microwave – Ping! Women are more like Crock-Pots: they are not stimulated by sight and they take a while to heat up. A woman needs words, gestures, flowers and so many prerequisites to sex. All a man needs is to see something and he is ready. These differences create an incredible avenue for misunderstanding. Here is the good news, though: I have found the solution and it has worked wonders in my sex life.

What I have found is that there is a solution that works and it is incredibly simple but hard to notice. Early in my marriage I went through the same frustration that many men go through. I wanted sex all the time and I could not figure out why my wife did not also want sex all the time. I was frustrated. When a man does not get sex, everything around him is off. He might kick the dog, growl at the kids, punch the refrigerator, and refuse to smile. Men, I am sure you want to know what I discovered to solve this problem. Here the answer: I call it "the formula." What is the formula, you may ask? Well, it is a compromise that enhances your sex life tremendously. After years of frustration I found out that men were expecting a full course meal when what they really needed was a "snack" to make them happy until the full course meal was available. A snack is sometimes referred to as a "quickie," where the wife makes sure that her husband experiences fulfillment even though she may not be "into it" at the time.

Wives have to understand how men are made up and what helps to achieve a happy marriage in order to ensure that this happens. Eventually I realized that while my wife needed lights, music, romance and everything else that goes with a wonderful night of intimacy, I did not need a full course meal; all I needed was a snack and then the world would seem much brighter: I would no longer kick the dog; I could smile at the kids; and everything would be fine. So whenever I was in need, my wife began to accommodate me for the purpose of making sure that I am satisfied. There would be times later for a more romantic sexual experience; but the snack was about meeting a real need. Once we discovered this, I became a happier person and she was happier because I was happy. This is one of the reasons that the Bible says we should not deprive each other (1 Corinthians 7:5).

So the snack (quick sex, no frills or excessive involvement by the wife) solves the problem of the sexually frustrated man. But we do not want to end there, because a woman needs to be fulfilled sexually as well, even though generally not as frequently.

Men, I have found a formula for making sure that your wife is fulfilled sexually as well. As stated previously women are stimulated differently; their sexual experience takes a long time to develop and they are more difficult to satisfy. So here are some of the things that I have learned are helpful in satisfying your wife sexually.

#1 – Small things

I have learned to take care of some things that are small to me but big to her. Women like to talk before sex, long before the act. So when she comes home I meet her at the door, invite her in, tell her to take off her shoes and ask her if she would like me to rub her feet. This allows us to converse while she is also being physically relaxed. Women need to be relaxed to have sex; men do not. While we are talking and I am massaging her feet, she gets to tell me about her day and I listen to her, which takes her mind away from the stress and helps her to enter another zone. It is important to listen. So now she is de-stressed. Next I help her if she needs help around the house. Remember, the less stress she has to deal with, the more relaxed she is. When we do go into the bedroom and she is already de-stressed, we take a bath or shower together, which further relaxes her, and I offer her a full body massage, head to toe. I find some relaxing music and keep talking while I am giving the massage.

#2 – COMMUNICATE

It is important to find out what a woman wants and prefers sexually, rather than assuming. When you are in bed you have to ask what stimulates her, and where she likes to be touched or kissed and how. You may also want to ask if you are doing it right, because the aim is to make sure she is pleased. Remember to take your time as a man and make sure you make every effort to satisfy her, because women require greater effort and take a longer time than a man to be satisfied. Once she is at the point of satisfaction, you can join in full throttle. If at all possible, make sure she achieves a climax first, or you simultaneously climax; because a man cannot please a woman after he has experienced a climax.

#3 – ROMANCE

Women are normally much more romantically inclined than men; so this is an area that we as men have to work on constantly: buying flowers, leaving her notes, sending her text messages or emails, taking her out to dinner or a movie or for a walk. Practice romantic gestures and, as I said earlier in this book, enlist help if you have a hard time figuring out what to do; read books, talk to friends who have it down to a science, and keep practicing. This tip probably should have been first on the list, but I think you get the picture.

#4 – ENJOY YOUR WIFE

Enjoy your relationship. Enjoy—not endure—your spouse. The Bible created marriage as an enjoyable journey; so you have to enjoy the journey. Sometimes we are always trying to fix problems; but at some point, we need to have a happy relationship, we need to have some happy times. The marriage needs to be fun. I thank God for my wife because we laugh together and we have a whole lot of fun. I am enjoying my marriage. She always insists that she is the one who causes the most laughter, and that's true. That's why I like to carry her wherever I go; she provides a level of joy for me, just as the Bible promised. The Bible says enjoy the wife of your youth (Proverbs 5:18). And of your old age too, for I am not a youth anymore.

You have to keep peace in your home. The final scripture I want to leave with you is Proverbs 5:15. Here's what it says: *Drink water from your own cistern.* It means you are not supposed to drink someplace else. So when you want to have a drink, look to your wife. If you do not have a wife, learn to acquire one, as the scripture says.

> *Should your fountains be dispersed abroad,*
> *Streams of water in the streets?*
> *Let them be only your own,*
> *And not for strangers with you.*
>
> *Let your fountain be blessed,*
> *And rejoice with the wife of your youth.*

God says that we are supposed to have joy in our relationships. Our marriage relationship is supposed to be a joy. If it is not a joy, it means you have some work to do; it does not mean you have to get out of it. Sometimes there may be some situations that are so complicated that you need counseling and similar help; but God wants you to work through the process until you can get to the joy. Proverbs 15 continues: *As a loving deer and a graceful doe, Let her breasts satisfy you at all times.* We tend to think of the Bible as the Holy Book with the Holy Word; but within it God gives you some assignments. He said, men, if you need breasts, let your wife's breasts satisfy you. I take those words literally and I make sure I do what it says. I enjoy my wife that God has given me in every way He said to enjoy her.

Proverbs 15 also says: *And always be enraptured with her love. For why should you, my son, be enraptured by an immoral woman, And be embraced in the arms of a seductress?* Here God says He has already provided you with all the fun that you need and He has provided you with a wife or a husband to enjoy; so you need to enjoy that relationship. Enjoy the wife of your youth; enjoy the husband of your youth. And enjoy the wife or husband of your old age, because sometimes people may think they can enjoy only the wife of their youth. You enjoy your wife of any age because as long as you're alive she's yours—God gave her to you; God gave him to you. You have to enjoy that relationship.

Enjoying your marriage also means enjoying activities together. You have to schedule alone time together and you have to make sure that the joy of the Lord is in your relationship. He came that our joy may be full (John 16:24). There needs to be some joy in the relationship; and sometimes you have to work at bringing that joy. I thank God that my wife and I came to a point in our relationship many years ago where we had a level of joy. That level of joy keeps increasing because we keep working on the relationship. And that's what we all must do. We all must continue to work on our relationship until it produces joy.

We want end on this last point; but just before we do, I want to mention something. A casual relationship with God opens the door to a bad spiritual connection. That's why it is important to have a passionate relationship with God. One of the keys to my success is that I do not play when it comes to God. I am not halfway in and halfway out. This is my life. I've been rescued and saved. When you find a good thing, you have got to stick with that good thing. People have found all kinds of solutions in life but the only thing that saved me was my relationship with Jesus Christ, so that's how I am rolling.

Money & Marriage

Chapter 15

Money

Pastor Dave:

As mentioned previously, the two things that are most associated with marital unrest are sex and money. We dealt with the sex part in the previous chapter; now let us deal with the money part. Many marriages break up not because of love or sex but because of disputes about money. Often the disputes could have easily been resolved if both parties understood how to handle money and agreed to work together. The first mistake that some couples allow is not having an agreed budget. If there is a budget then the budget would serve as a guide to spending, indicating what is allowed and not allowed. Many couples do not have a budget, do not have a priority list.

One of the keys to success is to have a budget first and then to break the budget into categories. You should begin with what I call an essentials budget. This consists of the expenditures for the things you need to survive, such as rent or mortgage, utilities, car, etc. If you don't make rent or mortgage a priority, for example, you might spend money on a new dress or new tennis shoes and have nowhere to live. So **begin with the essentials.** Once the essentials are taken care of, you move down the priority list until you get to discretionary items. Discretionary items are the things you purchase if you have extra income after the essentials are taken care of. This sounds simple, but I have met many couples who have no budget.

Continuing with the budget, we now look at who is responsible for each part of the budget. In some relationships, all the money is pooled and one or both parties monitor the expenditures. In other relationships, each individual is given items to cover based upon their level of income. Either method can work depending on the level of responsibility and accountability that each partner is capable of.

It is essential that you document your budget. Use a budgeting program, if possible, such as Quicken or some other budgeting software. The value of a money management software is that once you've entered your income and expenditure into the system, you can readily access these figures and retrieve historical information.

Discipline is key when it comes to money matters. **Neither person should spend unallocated money; and essentials money should not be spent on discretionary items.** For example, if the rent or mortgage is unpaid, you should not be buying a new TV or personal luxury item. My wife and I found that it worked best when we allocated expenses to be paid from individual budgets as opposed to a single budget. The main reason for this is that we had one checkbook in the beginning and there were times when one of us (mostly me) would forget to record expenditure and the balance anticipated was not what was available. It is important to determine what works best in your situation and not be hard and fast about a particular method.

Sometimes one party is better than the other at budgeting. In that case, that person should drive the budget exercise and explain to the other party via documentation how money was spent or allocated. It is important, and in fact essential, to determine beforehand what are the essential items, priority items, and discretionary items. The Bible asks us to consider how two people can walk together if they are not in agreement. This means that to move forward there should be a consensus about what to do with money. Beyond income and expenditure, decisions such as how much to save and how much or in what to invest are key. If, as a couple, you find difficulty with the process, it may be good to sit with a financial advisor or counselor who can assist and mediate where necessary.

I believe it is essential that you purchase and read books on money management from a Christian or Kingdom perspective. There are many resources available that show you how to budget, how to invest, how to save money, and how to grow financially. Take the time to read, get counsel, and seek a financial advisor; because if you do so, you can save yourself a lot of harm. Financial seminars are also a great tool to acquire additional knowledge.

Semi-Final Words

I SAY SEMI-FINAL words because this book is the first in a series that my wife and I will be producing on keys to success in marriage. The advice given to this point comes from our experiences during many years of marriage. But we have touched only some of the keys we have learned over the years.

Always remember the goal of the relationship. You chose to be together for a reason. Always keep your original goal in mind. In the course of a marriage there will be many difficult issues to navigate and you can either learn or burn from your issues. If you don't keep the main goal in mind, the small things will deter you and induce failure. The Bible declares that what God has joined together, let no one put asunder. This means that if you came together under God, do not let temporal issues divide you.

Action Steps

1. HABIT: We know that it takes twenty-one days to form a habit, but let's start with seven. Every day for the next seven days say something nice to your wife. Let me give you some hints of what to do if you are bashful and do not want to say something to her. Go ahead and write a note and put it in her purse, in the medicine cabinet on the counter where she cooks or where she fixes her makeup, or put it in her shoe.

2. ROMANCE: Practice romance; and if you are not sure what to do, seek assistance from books, the Internet, your children, or friends who are better at romance.

3. Practice welcoming your wife when she comes home, taking off her shoes and rubbing her feet while she tells you about her day.

4. LOVE LANGUAGES: Make it a point to learn and begin to practice the love language of your spouse: **QUALITY TIME, PHYSICAL TOUCH, ACTS OF SERVICE, GIFTS,** and **WORDS OF AFFIRMATION.**

5. **Make sure you communicate in affirming ways, using the least abrasive language.**

6. **Remind yourself to accept your spouse, including their faults.**

7. **Keep the 80/20 rule in mind. Do not let the 20 percent you dislike overshadow the 80 percent that you do like about your spouse.**

8. **Practice your caring skills, including opening doors for your wife, holding her hand in public.**

9. **Practice caring for your husband by doing things he likes—cooking a favorite meal, ironing his clothes.**

10. **Identify and work on triggers—things that generate a negative reaction—and learn to avoid triggers.**

11. **Practice forgiveness, even when you are right, because a soft answer turns away wrath and forgiveness is good for the soul. Men, practice nonsexual touching so that your wife can feel that her need for affection is being met outside of sex.**

12. **Remind yourself that progress is better than perfection and identify progress in your spouse. Compliment your**

spouse on the progress they make in their development or correction.

13. Remember to look for resolution rather than retribution. Seek to resolve rather than retaliate.

14. Make sure you establish boundaries for access of friends and associates of the opposite sex.

Make sure you never discuss your spouse's faults with friends.

Practice learning your spouse's nonverbal communications.

Implement the sex "formula" to ensure a healthy sexual relationship.

Implement a budget and review your budget monthly.

Recommended Readings on Marriage

- *Single, Married, Separated: Life After Divorce* – Dr. Myles Munroe

- *Understanding the Purpose and Power of Men* - Dr. Myles Munroe

- *Understanding the Purpose and Power of Women* - Dr. Myles Munroe

- *The Purpose and Power of Love and Marriage* - Dr. Myles Munroe

About the Authors

Dr. Dave Burrows currently serves as Senior Pastor of Bahamas Faith Ministries International which was founded by the late world renowned visionary and leader Dr. Myles Munroe whom he succeeded. Dr. Burrows is a multifaceted movtiator, inspirator, buisnessman, consultant and mentor. Dr. Burrows was a longtime close associate of Dr. Munroe for over 30 years having travelled and partnered with Dr. Munroe in many events and venues.

One of the foremost authorities in the world on Youth development and Youth Ministry and a lifelong Youth Ministry and Family ministry specialist with over 30 years of experience in Youth development, training and mentoring Pastor Dave has pioneered many successful programs for youth and families affecting gangs, youth from all backgrounds, youth leaders around the world, Churches, Pastors and entire organizations and denominations.

He previously served as an advisor to the Bahamas Government on Youth matters as Chairman of the National Youth Advisory Council on three occasions. In addition to serving in his current capacity, Dr. Burrows also serves as President of Dave Burrows Youth and Family International, Youth Alive Ministries and as founder and president emeritus of The Christian Youth Leaders Network and the Global Youth Ministry Leadership Network.

Affectionately known as "Davy B" or "The Ruffneck Pastor" Dr. Dave Burrows was Born and raised in The Bahamas as a troubled teenager involved in the street world of drugs, sexual promiscuity, violence and crime. While in College, through the influence of his brother-in-law Pastor Robyn Gool Dave made a complete turnaround and went on to graduate from Oral Roberts University with a degree in Social Work and minor in Business.

An accomplished author Dr. Burrows has published fourteen books, served as executive producer of five movies and three music soundtracks. His works include The Laws of Good Success, Making the Most of Your Teenage Years, Power of Positive Choices, Sex and Dating and Kingdom Parenting which he co-authored with Dr. Munroe . He has appeared on many local and international television programs and events hosted by TBN, TD Jakes Potters Touch, Oral Roberts University, Messiah College, Armstrong Williams, CBN Turning Point, The Potters House Denver, Dr. Fred Price and many others. He has spoken and conducted seminars extensively in the United States, Caribbean, Canada, Europe and Africa.

In addition to Youth and Family ministry Dr. Burrows has served as a business and technology consultant for many organizations. His clients have included corporations, civic and social organizations and churches. He previously served for many years as Vice President of both Bahamas Faith Ministries International and Myles Munroe International a global entity founded by the late Dr. Munroe. He founded and serves as president and CEO of Megabyte Computers and One Rib Publications.

Dr. Burrows has mentored and coached many individuals to personal and business success and continues to serve as both an inspirational and motivational speaker and life coach.

Contact Information:
dburrows@bfmmm.com
www.daveburrowsministries.com
pastordaveburrows@hotmail.com
242-461-6475 | 954-603-7285 | 242-327-0105

About the Authors

ANGELA BURROWS, a native of Nassau, Bahamas is a wife, mother, professional and a minister of the gospel. Her newest role is assisting her husband Dr. Dave Burrows as Senior Pastor of Bahamas Faith Ministries, founded by Dr. Myles Munroe.

Angela came to know Christ as a teenager and shortly after completing high school chose to continue her education at Oral Roberts University, in Tulsa, Oklahoma where she majored in Social Work. After returning to the Bahamas she got married and began working in the field of social work until entering the insurance industry where she flourished, climbing the industrial ladder to the rank of Vice President of Customer Service and Administration for Atlantic Medical, a company formerly owned by Travellers Insurance.

In 2000 Angela felt a need to invest more of her efforts into family pursuits as well as her family's businesses Megabyte Computers and One Rib Publications. She served as company administrator and overseer for more than 15 years. Both companies saw exponential growth under her management.

Angela has a heart for women and young people and served as a youth leader for more than 20 years at Bahamas Faith Ministries while her husband was youth pastor. She served as Vice President for Women of Excellence, the women's ministry at BFM. She has served as a mentor to many women, young and old. Her living room has been the therapists office and prayer room for many a young person over the years.

She is an accomplished speaker, loved for her quick wit, and concise yet colorful approach. She has travelled to the USA, United Kingdom, the Caribbean and Africa and shared with thousands of believers over the years. She has hosted numerous events, workshops and retreats for youth and families and most recently co-founded the Dave Burrows Youth and Family Center a non-profit organization focused on reaching troubled teens and families, subsidized in part by the Ministry of Education.

She frequently travels with her husband for ministry and has two adult children, Arri and Davrielle.

Contact Information:
Angieangel28@hotmail.com
pastordaveburrows@hotmail.com
www.daveburrowsministries.com
242-327-0105 | 242-461-6475

KEYS TO MARRIAGE SUCCESS

ANSWERING THE MOST IMPORTANT QUESTIONS ABOUT MARRIAGE

DVD

DR. DAVID & ANGIE BURROWS
PLEASING GOD
in Relationships
HOW TO KEEP
HEALTHY
RELATIONSHIPS

DAVID BURROWS

FROM THE SEX AND DATING SERIES

Horizontal Relationships